The IQ Workout Series

THE COMPLETE BOOK OF INTELLIGENCE TESTS

Philip Carter

WILEY

Copyright © 2005 by Philip Carter

Published by John Wiley & Sons Ltd, The Atrium, Southern Gate, Chichester, West Sussex PO19 8SQ, England

Telephone: (+44) 1243 779777
Email (for orders and customer service enquiries): cs-books@wiley.co.uk
Visit our Home Page on www.wileyeurope.com or www.wiley.com

Reprinted November 2006, July 2007

Philip Carter has asserted his rights under the Copyright, Designs and Patents Act, 1988, to be identified as the author of this work.

All Rights Reserved. No part of this publication may be reproduced, stored in a retrieval system or transmitted in any form or by any means, electronic, mechanical, photocopying, recording, scanning or otherwise, except under the terms of the Copyright, Designs and Patents Act 1988 or under the terms of a licence issued by the Copyright Licensing Agency Ltd, 90 Tottenham Court Road, London W1T 4LP, UK, without the permission in writing of the Publisher. Requests to the Publisher should be addressed to the Permissions Department, John Wiley & Sons Ltd, The Atrium, Southern Gate, Chichester, West Sussex PO19 8SQ, England, or emailed to permreq@wiley.co.uk, or faxed to (+44) 1243 770620.

This publication is designed to provide accurate and authoritative information in regard to the subject matter covered. It is sold on the understanding that the Publisher is not engaged in rendering professional services. If professional advice or other expert assistance is required, the services of a competent professional should be sought.

Other Wiley Editorial Offices

John Wiley & Sons Inc., 111 River Street, Hoboken, NJ 07030, USA

Jossey-Bass, 989 Market Street, San Francisco, CA 94103-1741, USA

Wiley-VCH Verlag GmbH, Boschstrasse 12, D-69469 Weinheim, Germany

John Wiley & Sons Australia Ltd, 33 Park Road, Milton, Queensland 4064, Australia

John Wiley and Sons (Asia) Pte Ltd, 2 Clementi Loop #02 01, Jin Xing Distripark, Singapore 129809

John Wiley & Sons Canada Ltd, 22 Worcester Road, Etobicoke, Ontario, Canada M9W 1L1

Wiley also publishes its books in a variety of electronic formats. Some content that appears in print may not be available in electronic books.

British Library Cataloguing in Publication Data

A catalogue record for this book is available from the British Library

ISBN 13: 978-0-470-01773-9 (PB)

Typeset in 11/14 pt Garamond by MCS Publishing Services Ltd, Salisbury, Wiltshire.

This book is printed on acid-free paper responsibly manufactured from sustainable forestry, in which at least two trees are planted for each one used for paper production.

Contents

Contents

1 Introduction

Intelligence may be narrowly defined as the capacity to acquire knowledge and understanding, and use it in different novel situations. It is this ability, or capacity, which enables the individual to deal with real situations and profit intellectually from sensory experience.

A test of intelligence is designed to formally study, under test conditions, the success of an individual in adapting to a specific situation.

There are a number of different methods which purport to measure intelligence, the most famous of which is the IQ, or intelligence quotient test. In the formation of such tests many psychologists treat intelligence as a general ability operating as a common factor in a wide variety of aptitudes.

Whilst many IQ tests measure a variety of different types of ability such as verbal, mathematical, spatial and reasoning skills, there is now a second school of thought in which it is believed that the earlier definitions of intelligence may be too simplistic.

It is now becoming increasingly recognised that there are many different types of intelligence and that a high measured IQ, although desirable, is not the only key to success in life. Other characteristics, such as outstanding artistic, creative or practical prowess, especially if combined with personal characteristics such as ambition, good temperament and compassion, could result in an outstanding level of success despite a low measured IQ. It is because of this that in recent years CQ (creative quotient) and EQ (emotional quotient), to name just two examples, have come to be regarded as equally important as, or even more important than, IQ measurement.

It should also be pointed out that having a high IQ does not mean that one has a good memory. A good memory is yet another type of intelligence, and could result in high academic success despite a low measured IQ test score.

The object of this book is to identify different types of intelligence and bring together tests for different aspects of intelligence into one book, and provide an objective assessment of abilities in a number of different disciplines.

This will, therefore, give readers the opportunity to identify their own strengths and weaknesses and thus enable readers to build on their strengths and work at improving their performance in areas of weakness.

As well as the identifying of such strengths and weaknesses, the tests and exercises in this book perform another important function, that of using and exercising the brain.

Despite the enormous capacity of the brain, we only use on average 2% of our potential brainpower. There is, therefore, the potential for each of us to expand our brainpower considerably.

It is important that we continually use our brain, for example, the more we practise at tests of verbal aptitude, the more we increase our ability to understand the meaning of words and use them effectively; the more we practise at mathematics, the more confident we become when working with numbers; and the more we practise our ability to move our fingers and manipulate small objects, the more dextrous we become at operations involving this type of aptitude.

Our brain is undoubtedly our greatest asset, yet, for most of us, it is the part of the body we most take for granted.

Our brain needs exercise and care in the same way as other parts of the body. We eat the right foods to keep our heart healthy, we moisturise our skin to keep it from drying out and, just as gymnasts strive to increase their performance at whatever level they are competing, by means of punishing training schedules and refinement of technique, there are exercises, or mental gymnastics, we can do to increase the performance of our brain and enhance quickness of thought.

Many people still have the outdated belief that there is little they can do to improve the brain they are born with and that brain cells continually degenerate with age, but in fact our brain cells continually develop new and stronger connections and adult brains can grow new cells, irrespective of age.

We should all be aware that we have the capacity to put our brain to even more use and unleash many hitherto untapped creative talents by continually exploring new avenues, experiences and learning adventures. By continually exploiting our enormous brain potential, we all have the ability to make more and stronger connections between our nerve cells, with the result that not only our mental but also our physical long-term well-being will improve.

Whilst the aim of the tests and exercises is therefore two-fold, that of identifying individual strengths and weaknesses and that of exercising the brain, they are at the same time, and equally importantly, designed to provide fun and entertainment to those who take them.

Aspects of intelligence

Although it is difficult to define intelligence, indeed it appears to have no formal definition, there is, nevertheless, at least one particularly apposite definition: *the capacity to learn and understand.*

Scores from standardised intelligence tests (IQ scores) are often used to define one's intelligence level. It is, however, becoming increasingly accepted that they do not reveal the complete picture and only provide a snapshot of a person's ability in the area under examination, so that, for example, someone who has scored highly on a verbal test can only be said to have a high verbal IQ and someone who has scored highly on a mathematical test can only be said to have a high numerical IQ. Obviously, therefore, the more different types of disciplines that are tested and examined, the more accurately the intelligence level of the individual can be assessed.

Whilst IQ testing is broadly based on the principle of a measurable and genetically inherited intelligence that is cast in stone for every individual and does not increase throughout adulthood, there is now another school of thought which believes there are many more different types of intelligences, some of which could be as a result of our upbringing and development and some of which could be the result of a natural talent with which we are born.

The concept of *general intelligence*, or *g*, was devised in the early twentieth century by the English psychologist Charles Spearman, who established *g* as a measure of performance in a variety of tests.

Spearman's research led him to the conclusion that the same people who performed well in a variety of mental tasks tended to use a part of the brain that he termed *g*. The *g* factor, therefore, laid the foundation for the concept of a single intelligence, and the belief that this single, and measurable, intelligence enables us to perform tasks of mental ability.

Recent studies have to a certain extent reinforced Spearman's theory, and research has found that the *lateral prefrontal cortex* is the only area of the brain where an increase in blood flow takes place when volunteers tackle complicated puzzles.

Despite this, Spearman's concept remains highly controversial and is becoming increasingly challenged by those who claim that the concept of a single overall intelligence is too simplistic.

At the same time, there is a body of research whose findings suggest that our mental ability is not determined by biological inheritance, but as the result of social factors such as education and upbringing.

Whilst IQ tests are, and will remain, helpful in predicting future performance or potential in many areas, they do not provide us with other information, such as the ability to connect with other people emotionally or perform creative tasks that involve the use of imagination.

Although most IQ testing only assesses what is termed 'general ability' in three categories of intelligence, numerical, verbal and spatial (abstract) reasoning, there are several other equally important and valuable intelligences that need to be recognised and developed.

The theory of multiple intelligence (MI) advocates that the traditional view of a single general intelligence, *g*, is too narrow and that humans have multiple intelligences. By expanding our definition of intelligence

Introduction

to include multiple intelligences, we can identify, appreciate and nurture more of our strengths.

This is important, as it would be as rare for any one individual to be endowed in all the different intelligences as it would for any one individual not to possess some kind of talent. We all tend to be aware of some of our abilities and limitations, for instance, some of us may be great musicians but completely hopeless when it comes to fixing a problem with our car; others may be championship-class chess players but would never be able to smash a tennis ball into the opposing player's court; and others may possess great linguistic and mathematical skills but feel completely at a loss trying to make small talk at social gatherings. The fact is that no-one is talented in every domain and no-one is completely incapable in every domain.

The originator of the theory of multiple intelligences, Howard Gardner, a professor of education at Harvard University, defines intelligence as the potential ability to process a certain sort of information. The different types of intelligence are for the most part independent of one another, and no type is more important than the other.

In all, Gardner identifies seven different types of intelligence. These can be summarized as follows:

1. *Verbal/linguistic*, e.g. lexical skills, formal speech, verbal debate, creative writing.
2. *Body/kinesthetic (movement)*, e.g. body language, physical gestures, creative dance, physical exercise, drama.
3. *Musical/rhythmic*, e.g. music performance, singing, musical composition, rhythmic patterns.
4. *Logic/mathematic*, e.g. numerical aptitude, problem solving, deciphering codes, abstract symbols and formulae.
5. *Visual/spatial*, e.g. patterns and designs, painting, drawing, active imagination, sculpture, colour schemes.
6. *Interpersonal (relationships with others)*, e.g. person-to-person communication, empathy practices, group projects, collaboration skills, receiving and giving feedback.

7. *Intrapersonal (self-understanding and insight)*, e.g. thinking strategies, emotional processing, knowing yourself, higher order reasoning, focusing/concentration.

Although aspects of it are included in several of the above categories; in addition to the above seven basic types of intelligence can be added *creativity*, which has sometimes been referred to as 'the eighth intelligence'.

Additionally, if creativity is the eighth intelligence, then *memory* must be the ninth, and both creativity and memory are explored and tested in detail in Chapters 4 and 6, respectively.

Whilst Spearman concluded that people who performed well at varying tasks tended to use the same part of the brain, *g*, Gardner asserts that each of the above intelligences is located in one or more particular areas of the brain. Some of the evidence for this belief is provided by the study of people who have suffered brain damage, either from strokes or other causes, and who may, for example, still be able to sing words despite having lost the ability to use expressive speech.

Although the jury may still be out on the debate as to whether the *g* factor, as gauged by IQ tests, is just one single general intelligence, or whether there are, as Gardner and others suggest, a set of independent mental domains, it would appear to be coming increasingly apparent that, as we learn more about the human brain and how different parts of the brain appear to generate different intelligences, the more compelling Gardner's theory becomes.

The main lesson to be learned from this is that people can be intelligent in many different ways. It is completely wrong to write off or even put down someone who has scored badly in an IQ test which, after all, has only provided us with one type of information about that individual. All of us have the potential for achievement in some kind of intelligence and we also possess the potential for improvement in many other areas.

Although there are types of intelligence that cannot be tested in a book, for example, aptitude at performing physical tasks or playing a musical instrument, in the chapters that follow as many different types of intelligence will be tested and explored as is feasible to do.

Intelligence quotient (IQ)

Intelligence quotient (IQ) is an age-related measure of intelligence level and is described as 100 times the mental age. The word 'quotient' means the result of dividing one quantity by another, and a definition of intelligence is mental ability or quickness of mind.

Such tests are based on the belief that every person possesses a single general ability of mind. It is this which determines how efficiently each of us deals with situations as they arise, and how we profit intellectually from our experiences. This ability of mind varies in amount from person to person, and is what intelligence (IQ tests) attempt to measure.

Generally such tests consist of a graded series of tasks, each of which has been standardised with a large representative population of individuals. Such a procedure establishes the average IQ as 100.

IQ tests are part of what is generally referred to as 'psychometric testing'. Such test content may be addressed to almost any aspect of our intellectual or emotional make-up, including personality, attitude and intelligence.

Psychometric tests are basically tools used for measuring the mind; the word 'metric' means *measure* and the word 'psycho' means *mind*. There are two types of psychometric test, which are usually used in tandem. These are *aptitude tests*, which assess your abilities, and *personality questionnaires*, which assess your character and personality.

In contrast to specific proficiencies, intelligence tests are standard examinations devised to measure human intelligence as distinct from attainments. There are several different types of intelligence test, for example, Cattell, Stanford–Binet and Wechsler, each having its own different scale of intelligence.

The Stanford–Binet is heavily weighted with questions involving verbal abilities and is widely used in the United States of America, and the Weschler scales consist of two separate verbal and performance sub-scales, each with its own IQ rating.

It is generally agreed by advocates of IQ testing that an individual's IQ rating is mainly hereditary and remains constant in development to about the age of 13, after which it is shown to slow down, and beyond the age of 18 little or no improvement is found. It is further agreed that the most marked increase in a person's IQ takes place in early childhood, and theories are continually put forward about different contributory factors, for example, it has been claimed recently, following research in Japan, that the playing of computer games by children, which involve a high degree of skill and agility of mind, have resulted in higher IQ measurement.

IQ Tests are standardised after being given to many thousands of people and an average IQ (100) established, a score above or below this norm being used to establish the subject's actual IQ rating.

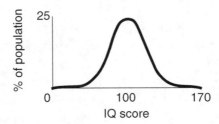

Because beyond the age of 18 little or no improvement in a person's IQ rating is found, the method of calculating the IQ of a child is different to the method used for an adult.

When measuring the IQ of a child, the subject will attempt an IQ test which has been standardized with an average score recorded for each age group. Thus, a child aged 10 years who scored the results expected of a child of 12 would have an IQ of 120, calculated as follows:

$$\frac{\text{mental age (12)}}{\text{chronological age (10)}} \times 100 = 120 \text{ IQ}$$

However, adults have to be judged on an IQ test whose average score is 100 and their results graded above and below this norm according to known scores. A properly validated test would have to be given to some 20,000 people and the results correlated before it would reveal an accurate measurement of a person's IQ.

Like most distributions found in nature, the distribution of IQ takes the form of a fairly regular bell-curve (see diagram above). On the Stanford–Binet scale, half the population fall between 90 and 110 IQ, half of them above 100 and half of them below; 25% score above 110; 11% above 120; 3% above 130 and 0.6% above 140. At the other end of the scale the same kind of proportion occurs.

The earliest known attempts to rank people in terms of intelligence date back to the Chinese Mandarin system, circa 500 B.C., when studying the works of Confucius enabled successful candidates to enter the public service. The top 1% of candidates were successful in progressing to the next stage, where they would again be run off against each other, and the procedure repeated yet again through a final layer of selection. Thus, the chosen candidates were in the top 1% of the top 1% of the top 1%.

The first attempt to measure scientifically the difference between the mental abilities of individuals was made by Sir Francis Galton in the nineteenth century, when he tried to show that the human mind could be systematically mapped into different dimensions.

The first modern intelligence test was devised in 1905 by the French psychologists Alfred Binet and Theodore Simon after they were commissioned by the French government to construct tests that would ensure no child be denied admittance to the Paris school system without formal examination. The pair developed a 30-item test, which included a wide range of different types of problems.

In 1916, the American psychologist Lewis Terman revised the Binet–Simon scale to provide comparison standards for Americans from age 3 to adulthood and the concept of the ratio of the mental age to chronological age, multiplied by 100, was added. Terman devised the term '*intelligence quotient*' and developed the Stanford–Binet intelligence test to measure IQ after joining the faculty of Stanford University as professor of education. The Stanford–Binet test was further revised in 1937 and 1960 and remains today one of the most widely used of all intelligence tests.

In the mid-nineteenth century psychologists used information-loaded tests to assess the intelligence of their clients. Later, psychologists introduced the concept of mental speed when assessing performance. Around 1930, Furneaux demonstrated that a relationship did exist between power, meaning the absolute difficulty of a problem, and speed, meaning the time a person required to solve it. By increasing the difficulty by 30%, you double the time required to solve it, but a 60% increase will lengthen the time five-fold.

The first IQ testing on a mass scale was carried out by the US army during the First World War. Personality tests or character tests soon followed, but in the 1920s and 1930s studies began to define more closely the general concept of intelligence. What emerged was recognition of fluid and crystallised intelligence. Fluid intelligence was measured by references to spatial items, such as diagrams, drawings or pegs, and crystallised intelligence was measured through language and number.

There are many different types of intelligence tests; however, a typical IQ test might consist of three sections, each testing a different ability, usually comprising verbal reasoning, numerical ability and diagrammatic, or spatial, reasoning. In order to assess your overall general ability, the questions in the test that follows are multi-discipline and include a mix of verbal, numerical and diagrammatic questions, as well as additional questions involving logical thought processes together with a degree of lateral thinking.

While it is accepted that IQ is hereditary and remains constant throughout life and, therefore, it is not possible to improve your actual IQ, one weakness of this type of testing is that it is possible to improve your performance on IQ tests by practising the many different types of question, and learning to recognise the recurring themes.

In subsequent chapters of this book, readers will have ample opportunity to test themselves in different areas of brain activity and to identify their strengths and weakness in specific areas of intelligence.

It must be emphasised that a person who is good at IQ tests is not necessarily capable of excelling at academic tests, regardless of how

Introduction

logical and quick-witted he/she is. Often motivation and dedication are more important than a high measured IQ rating. To score highly on an academic test requires the ability to concentrate on a single subject, obtain an understanding of it, and revise solidly in order to memorise facts prior to an examination. Often it is difficult for someone with a high IQ to do this because of an overactive and enquiring mind, which cannot direct itself on one subject for very long and forever wishes to diversify. Such a person would have to apply a high level of self-discipline in order to succeed at academic tests but, if able to apply this self-discipline, would be likely to obtain a high pass mark.

Because the test that follows has been newly compiled for this book, it has not been standardised, so an actual IQ assessment cannot be given. Nevertheless, a guide to assessing your performance is provided in the Answers section.

A time limit of 90 minutes is allowed for completing all 40 questions. The correct answers are given at the end of the test, and you should award yourself one point for each completely correct answer. You should not exceed the time limit, otherwise your score will be invalidated.

Where preferred, the use of a calculator is permitted on numerical questions, except where indicated.

Test 1.1 IQ test

1 The white dot moves two places anti-clockwise at each stage and the black dot moves one place clockwise at each stage. After how many stages will they be together in the same corner?

2

	72496	is to	1315
and	62134	is to	97
and	85316	is to	167
therefore	28439	is to	?

3 Put the following words into alphabetical order:

arthropod, artificer, arteriole, artichoke, arthritis, articular, artillery, arthritic

4 Which two words are most opposite in meaning?

imaginary, realistic, illegible, impracticable, radical, embellished

5 What numbers should replace the question marks?

2	6	3	7	?
6	3	6	3	?
3	6	3	6	?
5	2	6	3	?

6 Which group of letters is the odd one out?

CEFH   LNOQ   UWXZ
HJKN   PRSU   DFGI

7 Identify two words (one from each set of brackets) that form a connection (analogy) when paired with the words in capitals.

RESTRAIN (suppress, deny, conceal)
WITHHOLD (curb, reserve, conceal)

8  **?**

Which figure should replace the question mark?

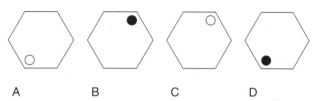

A   B   C   D

9 Spell out a 12-letter word by moving from letter to adjacent letter, horizontally and vertically (but not diagonally). You must find the starting point and provide the missing letters.

	C	A	I
C	L	O	D
N	E		E

10 What numbers should replace the question marks?

   100, 95, ?, 79, 68, ?, 40, 23

11 Associate is to colleague as accomplice is to:

   consort, friend, accessory, comrade, follower

12 Which is the odd one out?

   famous, illustrious, acclaimed, fabulous, noteworthy

13 What number should replace the question mark?

	7	
9	3	6
	2	

	5	
4	2	6
	1	

	13	
19	?	11
	5	

14 Which is the odd one out?

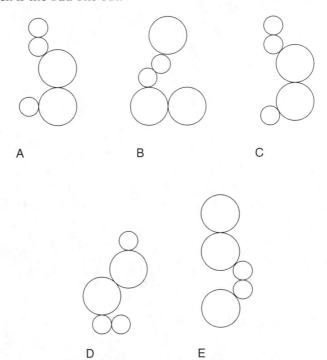

A   B   C

D   E

15 GAINED VOTE is an anagram of which two words that are similar in meaning?

16 What number should replace the question mark?

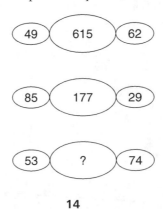

17 Which word in brackets is most opposite in meaning to the word in capitals?

MITIGATE (augment, palliate, appreciate, trust, destroy)

18

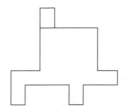

Which shape below is identical to the shape above?

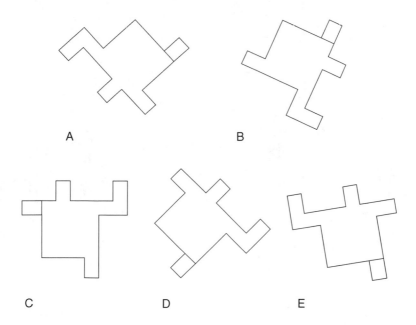

A   B

C   D   E

19 Which two words are closest in meaning?

educated, clear, literal, enervated, wordy, verbatim

20 What number should replace the question mark?

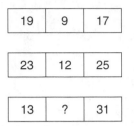

| 19 | 9 | 17 |

| 23 | 12 | 25 |

| 13 | ? | 31 |

21

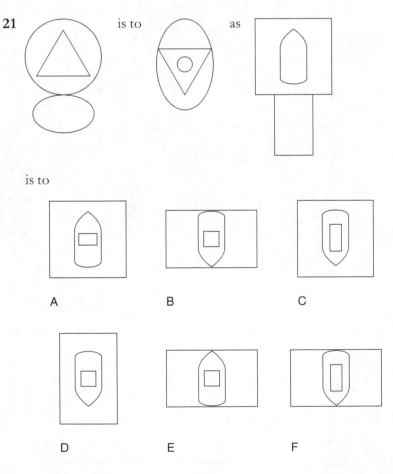

is to

A   B   C

D   E   F

22 What letter is three to the right of the letter immediately to the left of the letter which is four to the left of the letter G?

$$A \quad B \quad C \quad D \quad E \quad F \quad G \quad H$$

23 Which word in brackets is closest in meaning to the word in capitals?

HABITUATED (constant, accustomed, colonized, commonplace, energetic)

24

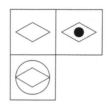

Which is the missing tile?

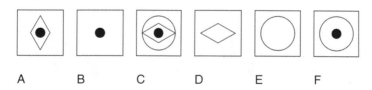

| A | B | C | D | E | F |

25 When full, a barrel of water contains 85 litres. How many litres remain after 40% has been used? (the use of a calculator is not permitted in this question).

26 DECISIVE LARK is an anagram of which two words that are opposite in meaning?

27

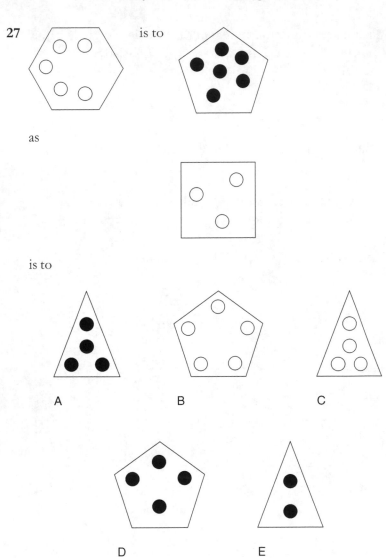

28 What number should replace the question mark?

0, 19, 38, 57, ?, 95

29

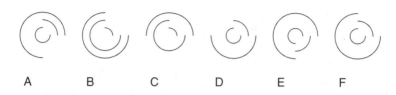

What comes next?

A   B   C   D   E   F

30 What number should replace the question mark?

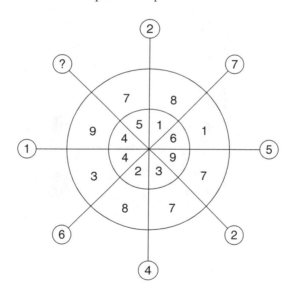

31 Switch A turns lights 1 and 2 on/off or off/on.
Switch B turns lights 2 and 4 on/off or off/on.
Switch C turns lights 1 and 3 on/off or off/on.

Switches A, C and B are thrown in turn, with the result that
Figure 1 turns into Figure 2. Which of the switches A, B or C
must, therefore, be faulty?

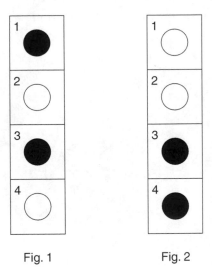

Fig. 1   Fig. 2

32 Which is the odd one out?

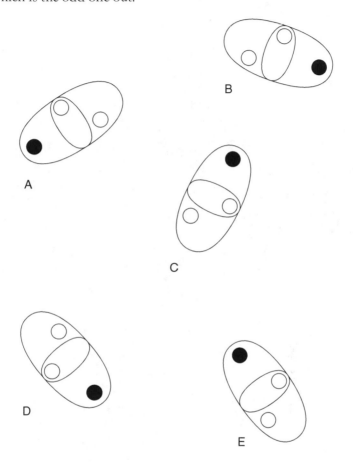

33 What number should replace the question mark?

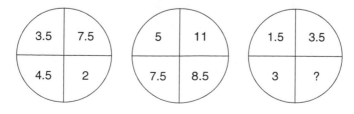

34

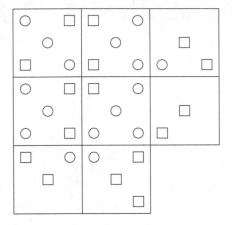

Which is the missing tile?

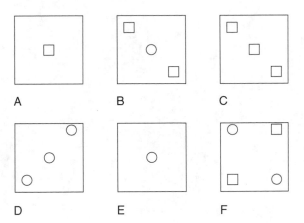

35 Start at one of the four corner letters and spiral clockwise round the perimeter, finishing at the centre letter to spell out a nine-letter word. You must provide the missing letters.

N	A	N
R		O
	T	C

36 What number should replace the question mark?

10, 21, 33, 46, 60, 75, ?

37

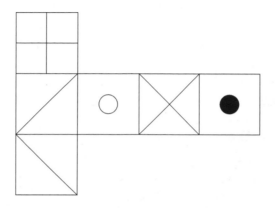

When the above is folded to form a cube, which is the only one of the following that can be produced?

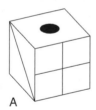 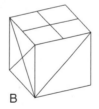 

A   B   C

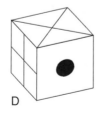 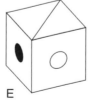

D   E

38 Joe has one and a half times as many as Mo, and Mo has one and a half times as many as Flo. Altogether they have 76. How many has each?

39 Which one of the following sentences is correct?

- The Gardener's Association debated whether to hold it's bi-annual flower show at the beginning of April and September, or at the end of April and September each year.
- The Gardeners' Association debated whether to hold its biennial flower show at the beginning of April and September, or at the end of April and September each year.
- The Gardeners' Association debated whether to hold it's bi-annual flower show at the beginning of April and September, or at the end of April and September each year.
- The Gardeners' Association debated whether to hold its bi-annual flower show at the beginning of April and September, or at the end of April and September each year.
- The Gardener's Association debated whether to hold its biennial flower show at the beginning of April and September, or at the end of April and September each year.
- The Gardeners' Association debated whether to hold it's bi-annual flower show at the beginning of April and September, or at the end of April and September each year.
- The Gardener's Association debated whether to hold it's biennial flower show at the beginning of April and September, or at the end of April and September each year.

40 What number should replace the question mark?

1	3	7	13
4	6	10	16
9	11	15	21
16	18	22	?

2 Specific aptitude tests

In the somewhat complex area of psychometric testing, the terminology and procedures involved are sometimes misunderstood or misinterpreted.

The word 'aptitude' is often misused to mean ability or achievement, and in the context of psychometric testing aptitude may be regarded as just another way of referring to specific ability. There is, however, a subtle technical difference between the three words 'achievement', 'ability' and 'aptitude', which can be distinguished as follows:

Achievement – what you have accomplished in the past.

Ability – what you are able to demonstrate in the present.

Aptitude – how quickly or easily you will be able to learn in the future.

Psychometric tests can be broadly divided into two main categories:

1. Tests of *maximum* performance, such as ability or aptitude.
2. Tests of *typical* performance, such as personality or interest.

An ability test is designed to measure maximum performance and potential in a number of areas. These abilities can be measured separately, or combined to give an assessment of overall general ability. Often tests are constructed so that they relate to a specific job or skill and assess things such as perceptual speed or mechanical reasoning.

Examples of ability tests are; general intelligence tests (IQ tests), knowledge-based attainment tests and aptitude tests, which test the ability to use knowledge.

Ability is a very general term which can be applied to many different types of specific ability. There are, in fact, over 50 different human abilities, although these fall within the following four main categories:

1. *Cognitive reasoning* – verbal, numerical, abstract, perceptual, spatial, mechanical. A very broad and general definition of the word 'cognition' is: knowing, perceiving and thinking. It is studied by psychologists because it reveals the extent of a person's ability to think.
2. *Psychomotor* – eye and hand coordination.
3. *Sensory* – hearing, touch, sense, smell, sight.
4. *Physical* – stamina and strength.

There are nine different types of aptitude, which may be summarised as follows:

1. *General learning* – learn and understand, reason and make judgements, e.g. how well we achieve at school.
2. *Verbal aptitude* – general lexical skills; understanding words and using them effectively.
3. *Numerical aptitude* – general mathematical skills; working with numbers quickly and accurately.
4. *Spatial aptitude* – understanding geometric forms; the understanding and identification of patterns and their meaning, e.g. understanding how to construct a flat-pack piece of furniture from a set of instructions.
5. *Form perception* – studying and perceiving details in objects and/or graphic material. Making visual comparisons between shapes, e.g. inspecting an object under a microscope in a laboratory; quality inspection of goods in a factory.
6. *Clerical perception* – reading, analysing and obtaining details from written data or tabulated material, e.g. proof reading, analysing reports.
7. *Motor coordination* – eye and hand coordination. Making rapid movement response quickly and accurately, e.g. actually being

able to assemble the flat pack piece of furniture once you have understood how it should be done; being able to operate a keyboard quickly and accurately; sporting skills.

8. *Finger dexterity* – manipulating small objects quickly and accurately, e.g. playing a piano, sewing.

9. *Manual dexterity* – the skill of being able to work with your hands, e.g. painting and decorating, building things, operating machinery.

In the case of most aptitude tests there is usually a set time limit which must be strictly adhered to in order for the test to be valid, and there is usually an average score which has been standardised in comparison with a group of people who have taken the same test.

When taken under these conditions there may be up to five levels of test performance expressed in percentage terms in comparison with the average score established:

1. *Top 10% of population* – extremely high degree of aptitude.
2. *Top one-third (excluding top 10%)* – high degree of aptitude.
3. *A score obtained by one-third of the population* – average degree of aptitude.
4. *Lowest one-third* – below average.
5. *Lowest 10%* – minimal aptitude.

The tests that follow are divided into three main sections: verbal aptitude, numerical aptitude and technical aptitude. Several spatial aptitude tests are included in subsequent chapters, specifically Chapter 3 (Logical reasoning) and Chapter 4 (Creativity).

Because they have been newly compiled for this book, the tests have not been standardised in comparison to scores obtained by other groups. Nevertheless there is a guide to assessing your performance at the end of each test, and because the tests relate to specific aptitudes, the results will give you the opportunity to identify your own particular strengths and weaknesses.

Unless stated otherwise, you should award yourself one point for each completely correct answer.

Section I – Verbal aptitude

Mastery of words is seen by many as having in one's possession the ability to produce order out of chaos and because of this it is argued that command of vocabulary is seen as a true measure of intelligence, with the result that verbal tests are widely used in IQ testing.

Verbal reasoning tests are designed to measure basic verbal ability (the ability to understand and use words), and typically include spelling, grammar, word meanings, completing sentences, synonyms and antonyms.

The exercises that follow test basic verbal aptitude in a number of separate areas including synonyms, antonyms, analogy, odd one out and verbal comprehension. There are also two advanced tests, one of which is multi-discipline and one which is anagram-based.

For each test a performance assessment is provided. There is also a time limit specified for completing each test, which should not be exceeded otherwise your score will be invalidated.

Test 2.1 Synonym test A

A synonym is a word having the same, or very similar, meaning to another of the same language. Examples of synonyms are: select and choose, easy and elementary, inquire and probe.

Test A is a series of 20 questions designed to test your knowledge of language and your ability to quickly identify words that have the same or very similar meanings. In each case choose just one word from the five words inside the brackets that is closest in meaning to the word in capitals.

You have 20 minutes in which to solve the 20 questions.

1 GLUTINOUS (churlish, adhesive, hungry, bright, desolate)

2 ILLUMINATING (real, authentic, informative, rational, coherent)

3 ESPOUSAL (avoidance, outburst, care, adoption, crux)

Specific aptitude tests

4 SIGNIFY (connote, outline, depict, welcome, influence)

5 ERUDITE (ancient, scholarly, distinguished, careful, itinerant)

6 IRRATIONAL (intransigent, irredeemable, unsafe, lost, nonsensical)

7 MODERATION (reticence, equanimity, humility, care, delicacy)

8 PANORAMIC (extensive, picturesque, distant, ceremonial, equidistant)

9 WEB (erode, create, clothe, lattice, skirl)

10 SATIATE (follow, censure, undermine, veto, overfill)

11 THOROUGHLY (attentively, assiduously, long-winded, eagerly, prodigal)

12 COGENCY (grace, competence, prestige, force, speed)

13 DESIROUS (eager, eligible, worthy, fulsome, true)

14 SOJOURN (relief, holiday, breach, retirement, rest)

15 PETRIFY (bedevil, calcify, agitate, decline, coerce)

16 ENCAPSULATE (facilitate, imitate, captivate, epitomize, impede)

17 ADMONITORY (scolding, juvenile, acceptable, praiseworthy, flexible)

18 PRETENCE (premises, precept, diversion, charade, preponderance)

19 FULMINATION (business, tirade, scripture, casket, channel)

20 WONT (awe, tribulation, perception, custom, desire)

Test 2.2   Synonym test B

Synonym test B is a series of 20 questions designed to test your knowledge of language and your ability to quickly identify words that have the same or very similar meanings. In each case choose just the two words from the six words provided that are closest in meaning.

You have 20 minutes in which to solve the 20 questions.

1 chop, gnaw, grate, sever, chew, destroy

2 inimitable, corresponding, matchless, surpassed, mature, imposing

3 delegate, advise, identify, recruit, adjust, mobilise

4 boorish, unchaste, stable, impure, unjust, bizarre

5 workaday, prosaic, feasible, easy, special, effective

6 unassailable, kind, inveterate, entrenched, contrary, convoluted

7 truncate, abandon, misuse, relinquish, rectify, denounce

8 snappish, ordinary, cursory, shrewd, sardonic, hurried

9 severe, opinionated, crude, dogmatic, unprincipled, vocal

10 progress, orbit, travel, run, encircle, align

11 orchestrate, display, employ, defeat, sustain, score

12 conspicuous, virulent, wild, profane, noxious, rancorous

13 just, somewhat, yet, once, now, moreover

14 elegant, serene, sophistic, shameful, sincere, fallacious

15 alter, assist, educate, facilitate, dream, cultivate

16 horizontal, unconscious, encompassed, submissive, supine, feral

17 farm, fare, style, food, firm, variety

18 guide, shepherd, farmer, shelter, carry, relocate

19 retreat, conclude, alight, circulate, call, getaway

20 intellect, symbol, rank, savour, genre, type

Test 2.3   Antonym test A

An antonym is a word with the opposite meaning to another of the same language. Examples of antonyms are big and small, true and false, happy and sad.

Test A is a series of 20 questions designed to test your knowledge of language and your ability to quickly identify words that have opposite meanings. In each case choose just one word from the five words inside the brackets that is most opposite in meaning to the word in capitals.

You have 20 minutes in which to solve the 20 questions.

1 CHECK (stay, accelerate, monitor, foil, win)

2 INVARIABLE (valueless, viable, genuine, flexible, simple)

3 RIBALD (genteel, attractive, serious, ethical, austere)

4 TOUCHY (obedient, fortunate, genial, sympathetic, durable)

5 TOTALITARIAN (democratic, fair, political, partial, conservative)

6 UNACCOUNTABLE (desirable, honest, potent, comprehensible, absolute)

7 WIDEN (prevent, compress, encase, hinder, terminate)

8 WORKABLE (atypical, amateurish, unfair, inconceivable, garrulous)

9 BRUTAL (civil, humane, patient, varying, happy)

10 PRODIGIOUS (tiny, tight, unproductive, inept, preposterous)

11 REMOTE (abstract, vital, related, astute, adjacent)

12 HYPOTHETICAL (academic, cagey, proven, punative, impressive)

13 IMMATURE (old, mundane, wise, mellow, respected)

14 EARTHLY (ethereal, temporal, seasoned, sensual, natural)

15 DENIGRATE (acknowledge, welcome, enhance, eulogise, master)

16 PUSILLANIMOUS (bold, cold, pure, sweet, dry)

17 COMPOSED (divided, nervous, specific, problematic, unhappy)

18 ASSET (acquisition, tragedy, misfortune, burden, mistake)

19 INTRINSIC (elemental, useless, obscure, unnecessary, appended)

20 MUSICAL (discordant, loud, lyrical, verbal, euphonious)

Specific aptitude tests

Test 2.4   Antonym test B

Antonym test B is a series of 20 questions designed to test your knowledge of language and your ability to quickly identify words that have opposite meanings. In each case, choose just the two words from the six words provided that are most opposite in meaning.

You have 20 minutes in which to solve the 20 questions.

1 wet, murky, cheerful, bright, still, happy

2 scarce, unwise, profuse, moral, ample, absent

3 contradict, continue, promote, intensify, quell, substantiate

4 fatuous, irrelevant, similar, therapeutic, contrary, rash

5 rigid, fluent, baroque, faltering, bare, effective

6 saturation, remuneration, tradition, reflection, salvation, perdition

7 eerie, hazardous, secure, active, restrained, sad

8 wise, foolproof, enlarged, wasteful, frugal, weak

9 candid, lucid, ignorant, angry, subtle, strong

10 sparse, gregarious, unsociable, graceful, weak, confused

11 litigate, allow, proffer, spread, proscribe, disagree

12 bob, rear, train, sail, bow, genuflect

13 important, rich, free, elevated, petty, perverse

14 neglected, brief, diplomatic, palpable, rude, devious

15 capture, absolve, captivate, diminish, hide, convict

16 climax, liking, zest, flavour, apathy, reluctance

17 trouble, turmoil, drivel, joy, passion, calm

18 elastic, severed, taut, level, slack, pliant

19 popinjay, neophyte, instructor, gambler, prize-fighter, aviator

20 humane, phlegmatic, erudite, solid, animated, healthy

Test 2.5   Analogy test A

An analogy is a similitude of relations where it is necessary to reason the answer from a parallel case. Questions may take the form 'A is to B as C is to?', as in the following example:

HELMET is to protection as TIARA is to:

adornment, queen, hair, royalty, head

Answer: adornment; both a helmet and a tiara are worn on the head, however, a helmet is worn for the purpose of protection and a tiara is worn for adornment.

You have 30 minutes in which to solve the 20 questions.

1 digital is to numbers as analogue is to:

symbols, hands, time, register, chronometer

2 concept is to notion as fixation is to:

obsession, idea, intuition, apprehension, proposition

3 confound is to bewilder as astound is to:

surprise, confuse, startle, astonish, horrify

Specific aptitude tests

4 corolla is to petals as pedicel is to:

    flower, stalk, root, leaves, anther

5 limerick is to five as sonnet is to:

    four, eight, twelve, fourteen, sixteen

6 laser is to beams as strobe is to:

    intensity, flashes, signals, X-rays, lamps

7 venerable is to august as lofty is to:

    imposing, December, magisterial, rarefied, grand

8 haematite is to iron as galena is to:

    enamel, copper, tin, zinc, lead

9 trireme is to ship as triptych is to:

    spear, stand, pattern, panel, play

10 east is to orient as west is to:

    aoristic, occident, orison, ottoman, ocean

11 artist is to brush as scribe is to:

    paper, pen, book, words, page

12 squander is to waste as employ is to:

    exploit, obtain, benefit, consume, use

13 stopcock is to pipe as throttle is to:

    valve, engine, flow, machine, regulate

14 Aries is to ram as Cygnus is to:

   goat, fish, swan, eagle, charioteer

15 continue is to resume as continuous is to:

   perseverance, unbroken, everlasting, repetition, persist

16 jade is to green as sapphire is to:

   blue, red, black, brown, yellow

17 tangent is to touch as secant is to:

   meet, divide, coincide, intersect, join

18 cleaver is to cut as auger is to:

   drill, chop, hammer, shape, saw

19 competent is to skilful as adept is to:

   capable, expert, able, clever, knowledgeable

20 aspiration is to ambition as fruition is to:

   realisation, success, victory, recognition, desire

Test 2.6   Analogy test B

In each of the following, identify two words (one from each set of brackets) that form a connection (analogy) when paired with the words in capitals, e.g:

   CHAPTER (book, verse, read)
   ACT (stage, audience, play)

Answer: book and play; a chapter is a division of a book and an act is a division of a play.

Specific aptitude tests

You have 30 minutes in which to solve the 20 questions.

1 PLUM (eat, grow, fruit)
   WILLOW (leaves, tree, crop)

2 RIFLE (bullet, gun, fire)
   CATAPULT (project, fling, weapon)

3 FOX (tail, hunt, fur)
   PEACOCK (fly, plumage, breed)

4 EVENING (morning, night, day)
   AUTUMN (day, winter, season)

5 STELLATE (sword, star, triangle)
   TOROID (funnel, ring, crescent)

6 TASTE (food, swallow, tongue)
   WALK (run, legs, move)

7 CHEMISTRY (laboratory, reaction, substances)
   FAUNA (plants, animals, countryside)

8 TRAVEL (journey, map, list)
   ATTEND (meeting, programme, boardroom)

9 FOREWORD (read, progress, book)
   OVERTURE (music, opera, composer)

10 RESIGN (politician, leave, parliament)
    ABDICATE (rule, king, realm)

11 CASTOR (sugar, furniture, wheel)
    ROWEL (bicycle, hub, spur)

12 MOBSTER (gangster, criminal, prohibition)
BRIGAND (fugitive, bandit, desperado)

13 CLAVIER (piano, compose, instrument)
TAMBOUR (music, beat, drum)

14 QUADRUPED (four, year, animal)
QUATRAIN (verse, eight, ship)

15 LARGO (loud, solemn, slow)
PIANO (lively, soft, fast)

16 GLUTTONY (food, weight, sin)
CHARITY (philanthropy, kindness, virtue)

17 VESTRY (church, hospital, refuge)
DISPENSARY (monastery, laboratory, hospital)

18 MODIFY (correct, regulate, change)
REDRESS (adjust, align, rectify)

19 MOAT (ditch, portcullis, crater)
TURRET (rampart, watchtower, defence)

20 SAVANNAH (inlet, highland, grass)
SIERRA (ravine, mountain, rock)

Test 2.7 Classification test

In this test you are given a list of five words and are required to choose which of the five words is the odd one out. This may be for a variety of reasons, as in the following examples:

(a) calm, quiet, relaxed, serene, unruffled

Specific aptitude tests

Answer: 'quiet' is the odd one out, as the rest mean the same thing. However, your being quiet does not necessarily mean that you are calm, relaxed, serene or unruffled. You could be extremely upset and agitated but still remain quiet.

(b) abode, dwelling, house, residence, street

Answer: 'street' is the odd one out, as the rest are specific places in which we live. 'Street' is a general term which may contain many houses, gardens, trees, road surfaces, etc.

You have 30 minutes in which to solve the 20 questions.

1 erect, upright, perpendicular, level, vertical

2 unequalled, paramount, exceptional, unsurpassed, finest

3 case, coffer, crate, chest, covering

4 cajole, deceive, beguile, inveigle, persuade

5 visit, summon, invite, assemble, convene

6 synagogue, mosque, pagoda, steeple, cathedral

7 hogwash, buffoonery, gibberish, gobbledegook, mumbo-jumbo

8 satisfactory, perfect, acceptable, fine, suitable

9 quadrangular, cubic, rectangular, spheroid, square

10 discontinue, forgo, relinquish, surrender, abandon

11 parched, desiccated, scorched, barren, dehydrated

12 pamphlet, certificate, catalogue, brochure, leaflet

13 burrow, till, cultivate, furrow, harrow

14 simian, ape, feline, monkey, primate

15 design, hew, chisel, sculpt, fashion

16 imaginary, strange, visionary, illusory, unreal

17 fete, holiday, gala, jamboree, carnival

18 obliquely, laterally, sideways, crabwise, orbicular

19 submit, distribute, tender, proffer, offer

20 sporadic, periodic, erratic, occasional, recurrent

Test 2.8 Comprehension

Each of the three passages below has had 15 words removed which have been listed at random below each passage. In order to test your verbal skills and comprehension ability, you must restore the 15 words correctly into each passage.

You have 30 minutes in which to reconstruct the three passages.

1 Just as the _____ (1) _____ (2) was half-way through _____ (3) his most _____ (4) and difficult _____ (5), the _____ (6) thing that could have happened did, and all hell was let loose as Ben _____ (7) a cat through the dining room _____ (8). Apart from almost barking the house down and _____ (9) drowning out the second half of the question, Ben _____ (10) across the dining room in a _____ (11) blur before throwing _____ (12) against the _____ (13) door with a _____ (14) _____ (15).

window	question	himself	sickening	hapless
involved	worst	saw	shot	crash
asking	interviewer	totally	brown	kitchen

2 We all have the potential to be ____ (1), however, because of the ____ (2) of modern ____ (3) and the need for ____ (4), many of us never have the ____ (5) or opportunity, or indeed are given the ____ (6), to ____ (7) our ____ (8) talents, even though most of us have ____ (9) ____ (10) to ____ (11) this ____ (12) in the form of ____ (13) which has been fed into, collated and ____ (14) by the ____ (15) over many years.

sufficient	pressures	brain	realise	encouragement
ammunition	data	living	latent	time
processed	creative	potential	specialization	explore

3 ____ (1) is the ____ (2) of new ____ (3), and ____ (4) is the ____ (5) of this knowledge. The ____ (6) of learning and memory, therefore, is the ____ (7) of all our knowledge and ____ (8) and is what ____ (9) us to ____ (10) the ____ (11), ____ (12) in the ____ (13) and ____ (14) for the ____ (15).

abilities	plan	acquisition	basis	consider
learning	retention	combination	past	memory
future	enables	knowledge	present	exist

Test 2.9 Advanced verbal test A – multi-discipline

This test is a miscellaneous selection of 25 verbal questions designed to measure language use or comprehension and your ability to adapt to different types of question.

You have 60 minutes in which to solve the 25 questions.
You should read the instructions to each question carefully.

1 The school ____ tried to persuade the police not to ____ the boys for what had been a ____ lapse in their good behaviour.

Insert three of the following words into the passage in order for it to read correctly:

momentous, prosecute, principle, persecute, principal, momentary

2

	C	E
I		R
S	T	I

Start at one of the four corner letters and spiral clockwise round the perimeter, finishing at the centre letter to spell out a nine-letter word. You must provide the missing letters.

3

E	I	L	
	S	E	A
R	U	C	N

Work from letter to letter horizontally and vertically (but not diagonally) to spell out a 12-letter word. You must find the starting point and provide the missing letters.

4

	A	
I	L	H
S	M	I

Start at one of the four corner letters and spiral clockwise round the perimeter, finishing at the centre letter to spell out a nine-letter word. You must provide the missing letters.

5

R	E	A	T
	C	I	I
P	A	E	

Work from letter to letter horizontally and vertically (but not diagonally) to spell out a 12-letter word. You must find the starting point and provide the missing letters.

6

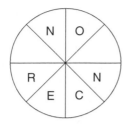 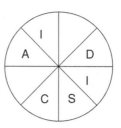

Find two eight-letter words, one in each circle, and both reading clockwise, that are synonyms. You must provide the missing letters.

7

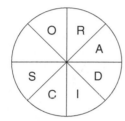 

Find two eight-letter words, one in each circle, and both reading clockwise, that are antonyms. You must provide the missing letters.

8 Change one letter only in each of the words below to produce a familiar phrase:

ACE TIE CART ON

9 Which word in brackets means the same as the word in capitals?

RAPACITY (avarice, affinity, envy, speed, euphoria)

10 Change the position of six words in the sentence below in order for it to make sense:

There is no considerable success of another, as what is considered to be success by one definition may differ single for individual.

11 Change the position of four words in the sentence below in order for it to make sense:

> When placed in marks, the question mark is used inside the quotation dialogue, and replaces the full stop.

12 Change the position of four words in the sentence below in order for it to make sense:

> The candidate was able to sustain his level to demonstrate a high ability of work activity.

13

L	L	B		
Y	T	I		
I	I	A	D	H
		E	N	C
		I	N	R

Each square contains the scrambled letters of a nine-letter word. Find the two words which are synonyms.

14 Place a word in the brackets that means the same as the definitions either side of the brackets:

> lean over to one side (_____) catalogue

15 Which two words that sound alike, but are spelled differently, mean:

> mode/estate

16

M	S	N		
A	N	O		
U	Y	O	I	N
		T	O	I
		N	G	C

Each square contains the scrambled letters of a nine-letter word. Find the two words which are synonyms.

17 clever is to ingenious as wise is to:

perspicuous, intelligent, astute, sagacious, resourceful

18 Identify two words (one from each set of brackets) that form a connection (analogy) when paired with the words in capitals:

EARTH (perigee, zenith, aphelion)
SUN (nadir, perihelion, conjunction)

19 Which two words are most opposite in meaning?

literal, zealous, risible, feral, fanciful, pervasive

20

D	A	
R		E
E	T	S

Start at one of the four corner letters and spiral clockwise round the perimeter, finishing at the centre letter to spell out a nine-letter word. You must provide the missing letters.

21

S	O	
	C	N
I	A	I

Start at one of the four corner letters and spiral clockwise round the perimeter, finishing at the centre letter to spell out a nine-letter word. You must provide the missing letters.

22 Which word in brackets is most opposite in meaning to the word in capitals?

QUERULOUS (undemanding, believable, orthodox, synthetic, dry)

23 Place a word in the brackets that means the same as the definitions either side of the brackets:

fall back on (_____) retreat

24 Below are seven synonyms of the keyword RIGID. Take one letter in turn from the seven synonyms to spell out a further synonym of the keyword RIGID:

harsh, rigorous, stern, stringent, severe, strict, set

25 Which two words are most opposite in meaning?

thrift, presage, introspection, profligacy, horde, parsimony

Test 2.10   Advanced verbal test B – anagrams

An anagram is a description of any of several types of word puzzle based upon the rearranging of letters in words. There are many variations on the basic theme, several of which are included in this test.

This test is designed to test your verbal dexterity and your knowledge of words, and the ability to spot different word patterns. It also requires you to think quickly and adapt your mind to each different style of question.

For example: SOFT LAWS is an anagram of which two words (4, 4) which are opposite in meaning? *Answer*: fast, slow

You have 75 minutes in which to solve the 20 questions.

1 SUP LIME is an anagram of which seven-letter word?

2 TAXI FEE PLOT is an anagram of which two words (4, 7) that mean the same?

3 STOUT APE is an anagram of which three-word phrase (3, 2, 3)?
(*Hint: page 205*)

4 Only one of the groups of five letters below can be rearranged to spell out a five-letter English word. Find the word:

    PCEOL   GRILN   NBDRA   BILPO

5 Only one of the groups of five letters below can be rearranged to spell out a five-letter English word. Find the word:

    HURPA   ATHOC   NFEOT   ECILP

6 Which of the following is not an anagram of an animal?

    OK DENY   HOG REP   SHE ELK   GARBED

7 Which of the following is not an anagram of a tree?

    RAP LOP   PC USER   HER CRY   STOREY

8 Only one of the groups of five letters below can be rearranged to spell out a five-letter English word. Find the word:

    JEABY   LIROW   CANTU   PEOTM

9 DUCK SLICER is an anagram of which two words (5, 5) that are opposite in meaning?

10 NEAT GLUT is an anagram of which eight-letter word?

11 Solve the anagram in brackets (eight-letter word) to complete a quotation by Louis Pasteur:

'Chance favours the (RED PAPER) mind.'

12 Solve the anagram in brackets (nine-letter word) to complete a quotation by Alexander Cannon:

'A small mind is (IS NOT BEAT). A great mind can lead and be led.'

13 ELITE LAVA is an anagram of which nine-letter word?

14 AUNT SAL is an anagram of which seven-letter word?

15 Use each letter of the phrase RAN KEENER FACTORY once each only to spell out three kinds of boat or ship.

16 Use each letter of the phrase ENABLE PITCHFORK once each only to spell out three kinds of professions.

17 SHOE COIN is an anagram of which eight-letter word?

18 GOOD CLARA is an anagram of which two words that are similar in meaning?

19 BEE STOOL is an anagram of which eight-letter word?

20 POLICE RAID is an anagram of which 10-letter word?

Section II – Numerical aptitude

We all require some numerical skills in our lives, whether it is to calculate our weekly shopping bill or to budget how to use our monthly income.

Numerical ability tests are designed to assess how well a person can reason with numbers. Questions within these tests may involve either straightforward mathematical calculation, or problems that require the application of logical thought processes.

In the case of numerical problem solving, the actual mathematical process involved may be quite basic; however, you are being assessed on your ability to apply your basic mathematical knowledge in order to correctly solve the problem as quickly as possible, and your ability to deal with problems in a structured and analytical way.

Numerical questions are widely used in IQ testing and, as numbers are international, numerical tests are regarded as being culture-fair or culture-free, so that they are free of any particular cultural bias and no advantage is derived by individuals of one culture relative to those of another.

Individual tests include mental arithmetic, number sequences and logical reasoning, all designed to test a person's aptitude/ability at mathematical calculation, identifying number patterns and the ability to reason with numbers.

Test 2.11   Number sequence test

In a numerical sequence test it is necessary to identify a pattern that is occurring in the sequence. The numbers in the sequence may be progressing, or they may be decreasing, and in some cases they may be both progressing and decreasing within the sequence. It is up to you to determine why this is occurring and to either continue the sequence or to provide a missing number within the sequence.

Fill in the missing number(s) indicated by the question mark(s) in each question.

A time limit of 20 minutes is allowed.
The use of calculators is not permitted in this test.

1 0, 1, 4, 9, 16, 25, 36, 49, ?

2 9, 18, 27, ?, 45, ?, 63

3 100, 96.75, 93.5, 90.25, 87, ?

4 0, 100, 6, 94, 12, 88, 18, 82, ?, ?

5 17, 34, 51, 68, ?

6 1, 1, 2, ?, 24, 120, 720

7 100, 98, 94, 88, 80, 70, ?

8 1.5, 3, 5.5, 9, 13.5, ?

9 100, 50, 200, 25, 400, ?

10 2, 5.75, ?, 13.25, 17, 20.75

11 100, 1, 97.5, 3.5, 92.5, 8.5, 85, 16, ?, ?

12 110, ?, 99, 81, 72, 63, 54, 45

13 1, 2, 3, 5, 7, 10, 13, 17, 21, ?, ?

14 5, 26, 131, 656, ?

15 1000, 971.4, 942.8, 914.2, 885.6, ?

16 1, 1, 3, 15, 105, ?

17 36, 72, ?, 144, 180, 216, 252

18 1, 1, 2.5, 3.5, 4, 6, 5.5, 8.5, ?, ?

19 1, 2, 6, 12, 36, 72, 216, ?, ?

20 14, 16, 28, 32, 42, 48, 56, 64, ?, ?

Test 2.12   Mental arithmetic

It is evident that mental arithmetic is not practised in today's education system to the extent that it was several years ago, when children would learn their multiplication tables so well off by heart that they could give the answer to sums such as 9 multiplied by 8 or 6 multiplied by 7 almost without thinking. Perhaps this is not completely surprising in view of the widespread use of calculators and computers; nevertheless, proficiency at mental arithmetic is a valuable asset to have at one's disposal and it is also an excellent way of exercising the brain.

The following is a mental arithmetic speed test of 30 questions, which gradually increase in difficulty as the test progresses. You should work quickly and calmly and try to think at all times of the quickest and most efficient way of tackling the questions.

You have 45 minutes in which to solve the 30 questions.

The use of a calculator is not permitted in this test and only the answer should be committed to paper, the object of the test being that all the working out is done in your head.

1 What is 9 multiplied by 8?

2 What is 126 divided by 3?

3 What is 15 multiplied by 11?

4 What is 45% of 300?

5 Multiply 7 by 12 and divide by 6.

6 Divide 56 by 8 and add 17.

7 What is 35% of 250?

8 What is $\frac{5}{8}$ of 240?

9 Multiply 15 by 6 and subtract 29.

10 What is $\frac{3}{4}$ of 92 plus 13?

11 Multiply 7 by 4 by 6.

12 Divide 52 by 4 and add 17 multiplied by 3.

13 What is 3206 divided by 7?

14 Add $32 + 8 + 18 + 25$.

15 What is 55% of 320?

16 What is $\frac{5}{9}$ of 270?

17 Which is greater, $\frac{5}{8}$ of 112 or $\frac{7}{8}$ of 88?

18 Add 5683 to 1729 and divide by 2.

19 Divide 672 by 12.

20 Subtract 369 from 1250.

21 Add $\frac{2}{5}$ of 90 to $\frac{5}{6}$ of 78.

22 Multiply 72 by 15.

23 What is $\frac{8}{40}$ expressed as a decimal?

24 Deduct 865 from 1063.

25 Multiply 694 by 11.

26 Multiply 86 by 9 and add to 13 multiplied by 6.

27 What is 1000 less $\frac{5}{9}$ of 117?

28 What is $5.9 + 6.8 + 7.34$?

29 Deduct 7.3 from 34.2.

30 Multiply 6.85 by 7.

Test 2.13 Working with numbers

This test is a battery of 20 questions designed to measure your ability to work with numbers and think numerically.

A time limit of 90 minutes is allowed.

The use of calculators is not permitted in this test; however, written calculations are permitted.

1 How many minutes is it before 12 noon if 68 minutes ago it was three times as many minutes past 10 a.m.?

2 Jack is three times as old as Jill, but in three years time he will only be twice as old. How old are Jack and Jill?

3 Mal is one-and-a-half times as old as Sal, and Sal is one-and-a-half times as old as Al. How old are Al, Sal and Mal if their combined ages total 114?

4 If Alice gives Susan £6.00 the money they each have is in the ratio 2 : 1; however, if Susan gives Alice £1.00 the ratio is 1 : 3. How much money have Alice and Susan each before they exchange any money?

5 Bill and Ben share flower pots in the ratio of 3 : 5. If Bill has 180 flower pots, how many has Ben?

6 Tom, Dick and Harry wish to share out a certain sum of money between them. Tom gets two-fifths, Dick gets 0.45 and Harry gets £21.00. How much is the original sum of money?

7

How long are the sides of a rectangle which has a perimeter of 70 units and an area of 276 square units?

8 The call centre received its highest number of enquiries between 3 p.m. and 4 p.m., which was 40% more than the 250 enquiries it received between 2 p.m. and 3 p.m. How many calls did the call centre receive between 3 p.m. and 4 p.m.?

9 If A = 3, B = 4, C = 6 and D = 7, calculate the following:

$$\frac{(C \times D) - (B \times C)}{(A + C)}$$

10 During the first week of a sale a suit originally costing £280.00 was reduced by 15%. At the beginning of the second week it was reduced by a further 10%. What was the final sale price?

11 If my taxi journey takes 23 minutes and my train journey takes 49 minutes longer, what is my total travelling time in hours and minutes?

12 In 7 years' time the combined age of my sister and her three children will be 92. What will it be in 4 years' time?

13 In a survey on the High Street on a Saturday afternoon, $\frac{5}{16}$ of women questioned had bought just cosmetics, $\frac{5}{8}$ had bought just clothing, while 115 women had just browsed and bought nothing. How many women had just bought cosmetics and how many had just bought clothing?

14 The average of three numbers is 19. The average of two of these numbers is 24. What is the third number?

15 Tins of carrots cost 4 pence (£0.04) more if bought individually than if bought in packs of 12. If a pack of 12 costs £5.76, what is the cost of seven tins bought individually?

16 A batsman is out for 26 runs, which raises his batting average for the season from 15 to 16. How many runs would he have had to have scored to raise his average to 20?

17 A greengrocer ordered 4500 items of fruit consisting of apples, oranges and plums in the ratio of 2 : 3 : 4, respectively. How many of each item did he order?

18 If I drive 210 miles, how long will the journey take if I drive at an average speed of 20 m.p.h. for 120 miles and an average speed of 30 m.p.h. for 90 miles, and have a 60 minute stop for refreshments mid-way through the journey?

19 If five men can build a house in 21 days, how long will it take seven men to build the house, assuming all men work at the same rate?

20 At a recent small town election for mayor, a total of 972 votes were cast for the four candidates, the winner exceeding his opponents by 52, 78 and 102 votes, respectively. How many votes were cast for each candidate?

Test 2.14   Advanced numerical aptitude test

This test brings together a variety of different types of questions designed to test your powers of calculation and computation and logical reasoning.

A time limit of 60 minutes is allowed for completion of the 15 questions.

The use of a calculator is permitted in this test in respect of questions 6, 7, 9, 11, 13 and 14 only, but written notes are permitted throughout.

1

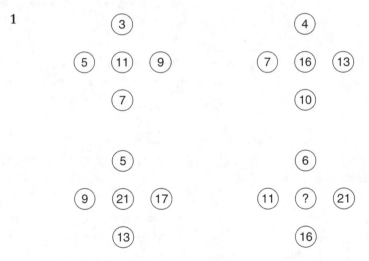

What number should replace the question mark?

2   A statue is being carved by a sculptor. The original piece of marble weighs 250 kg. In the first week 35% is cut away, in the second week 20% of the remainder is cut away and in the third week 25% is chiselled away and polished to produce the finished statue. What is the weight of the final statue?

3   10, 11, 9, 12, 8, 13, 7, 14, ?, ?

What are the next two numbers in the above sequence?

4 783 : 59
395 : 32
579 : 44
666 : ?

5 Three coins are tossed in the air at the same time. What are the chances that at least two of the coins will fall tails up?

6 A train travelling at a speed of 75 m.p.h. enters a tunnel that is 2.5 miles long. The length of the train is 0.25 miles. How long does it take for all of the train to pass through the tunnel, from the moment the front enters to the moment the rear emerges?

7

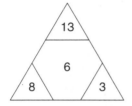

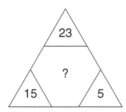

What number should replace the question mark?

8 10, 11, 14, 23, ?, 131

What number should replace the question mark?

9

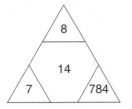

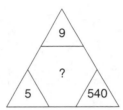

What number should replace the question mark?

10

7	8	4	19
3	14	5	22
2	7	?	27
12	29	27	?

What two numbers should replace the question marks?

11 I have collected 91 apples, which I wish to put into bags for handing out to some of my neighbours. All bags must contain the same number of apples and I wish to use as few bags as possible. How many neighbours received a bag of apples and how many apples did each bag contain?

12 I completed a journey by bus, rail and taxi. If the train fare cost £27.35, the taxi fare cost £15.90 less than the train fare and the bus fare cost £9.55 less than the taxi fare, how much did the total journey cost me?

13

What number should replace the question mark?

14 I have three rolls of turf, each measuring 20 metres long by 4 metres wide, with which I intend to cover two rectangular areas of ground, one of which is 6 metres by 18 metres and the other 15.5 metres by 5.5 metres. How many square metres of turf will I have left over?

15 Out of 144 guests at a conference, a quarter took their coffee with sugar only, $\frac{5}{8}$ took it with both milk and sugar, one out of every 16 guests took it with milk only and the rest took it black with neither milk nor sugar. How many guests took it black with neither milk nor sugar?

Section III – Technical aptitude

With the explosion of information technology, technical aptitude testing is becoming increasingly more important, as people with a higher scientific and technical aptitude have the potential to master technology much more effectively than someone with a lower technical aptitude. Employing job candidates who have displayed a high level of technical aptitude in technology-oriented jobs is, therefore, considerably more cost-effective, in terms of both training and efficiency of performance, in carrying out the job at the desired level.

As new technology continues to emerge and develop, it is important to employers that they have the means at their disposal to identify candidates who are able to learn these new technologies quickly and are able to apply these skills in order to solve complex problems in their jobs.

Test 2.15   Technical aptitude test

The following test consists of 15 questions that are designed to test your general scientific knowledge, technical aptitude and powers of mechanical reasoning and logic.

A time limit of 40 minutes is allowed.
The use of calculators is permitted in this test.

1

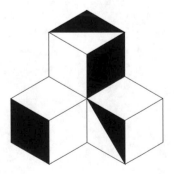

What percentage of the visible figure is shaded?

2

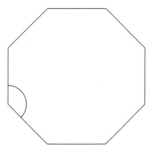

What is the value of the internal angle of an octagon?

3 Brass is an alloy made from two metals, _____ and _____ .

Which two metals are missing?

a) copper and iron
b) copper and tin
c) iron and tin
d) nickel and tin
e) iron and nickel
f) zinc and copper
g) iron and zinc

4

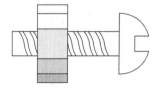

A nut is so tight on a screwed bolt you are having great difficulty unscrewing it. Which of the following is the most effective in freeing it?

a) cooling it
b) submerging it in warm water
c) heating it
d) none of the above

5

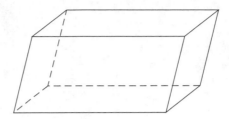

What is the name of the above figure?

a) icosahedron
b) rhombus
c) ellipsoid
d) parallelepiped
e) rhomboid

6

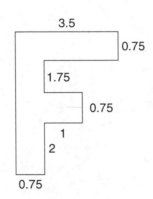

(not to scale)

What is the area in square units of the figure above?

7

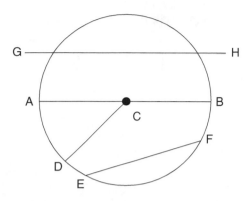

AB = _____ ; CD = _____ ; EF = _____ ; GH = _____ .

Given that point C is the centre of the circle, insert the names of the lines from the choice given below. One of the choices is not used:

secant, chord, radius, tangent, diameter

8 _____ is when heat travels from the warmed end of an object towards the cool end. _____ is when heat travels through space. _____ is when heat from a hotplate is transferred to water in a pan placed on the hotplate.

Insert the three types of heat below into their correct definition:

radiation, conduction, convection

9 Dynamism is the doctrine that all substance involves _____ .

Insert the correct word into the above definition from the choice below:

a) momentum
b) mass
c) force
d) motion
e) gravity

10 The speed of sound is approximately 740 m.p.h. A fire engine with its siren sounding is approaching you at 80 m.p.h. At what speed is the sound from the siren approaching you?

a) 820 m.p.h
b) 740 m.p.h
c) 660 m.p.h
d) 9.25 m.p.h

11

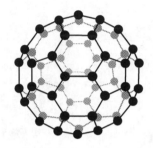

Buckminsterfullerine (as illustrated above) is a natural form, or allotrope, of carbon. It consists of 60 carbon atoms linked together to form an almost spherical C60 molecule. Which of the following does it consist of?

a) 24 hexagons and 8 pentagons
b) 12 pentagons and 20 hexagons
c) 30 hexagons and 10 pentagons
d) 16 hexagons and 12 pentagons
e) 20 hexagons and 12 pentagons

12

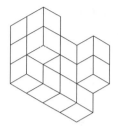

If you picked up a single cube, turned it around, and looked at it from all directions, six faces would be visible. If you picked up the figure above and looked at it from all angles and directions, how many faces would be visible?

13

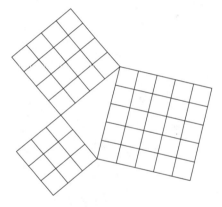

The above diagram is proof of which of the following?

a) Fermat's last theorem
b) Boyle's law
c) Pythagoras' theorem
d) Einstein's general theory of relativity
e) Godel's theorem
f) Euclid's algorithm
g) Coulomb's law
h) None of the above

14 In mathematical equations the order of operations is multiplication before addition. What is the value of ? in the following?

$$\{4[6 + (4 \times 9 + 14)]\} = ?$$

15 The _____ is a unit of frequency equal to one cycle per second.

Insert the correct word into the definition:

a) Joule
b) Hertz
c) diode
d) dyne
e) Kelvin

3   Logical reasoning

The *Concise Oxford English Dictionary* defines logic as 'the science of reasoning, proof, thinking or inference'.

In philosophy, logic (from the Greek *logos*, meaning word, speech or reason) is a science that deals with the principles of valid reasoning and argument. In this context, logic concerns only the reasoning process and not necessarily the end result. Thus, incorrect conclusions can be reached by so-called 'faulty' means if the original assumptions are faulty. There are many kinds of logic, such as fuzzy logic and constructive logic, which have different rules and different strengths and weaknesses.

A further definition of 'logical' is analytical or deductive, and this definition can be applied to someone who is capable of reasoning, or using reason, in an orderly, cogent fashion.

It is this latter definition with which we are concerned in this chapter and all the questions can be solved using this type of thinking process. There is no specialised knowledge required in order to solve them, just an ability to think clearly and analytically and follow a common-sense reasoning process step by step through to its conclusion.

Test 3.1   Pure logic

Test 1 consists of 10 questions of varying scope and difficulty. There is no specialised knowledge of mathematics or vocabulary required in order to solve these questions, just the ability to think clearly and analytically.

You have 50 minutes in which to solve the 10 questions.

1 elk
mink
mouse
gibbon
panther

Which creature comes next? Is it:

squirrel, tortoise, tigress, wildebeest, platypus or aardvark?

2 January
February
April
July
November
April
?

What comes next?

3

A	C
G	E

B	E
K	H

C	G
O	K

?	?
?	?

What letters should appear in the fourth square?

4

3	4	7	2	1	6
9	2	8	5	7	4
6	9	7	3	8	5
6	1	2	7	4	3
4	7	5	8	2	9
?	?	?	?	?	?

What numbers should appear on the bottom row?

5

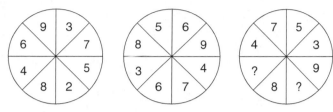

What numbers should replace the question marks?

6

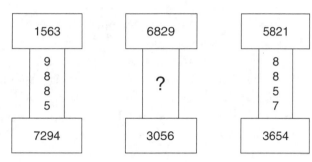

What number should replace the question mark?

7

7896432 is to 9872346
and 9247183 is to 4293817
therefore 8629471 is to ?

8 From the information already provided, find the link between the numbers in each row, and then fill in the missing numbers:

3859	1 1 1 4	— —
4978	— — — —	4 6
7579	— — — —	— —

9

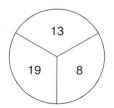
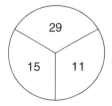
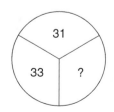

What number should replace the question mark?

10   3829718 is to 87283
            and 642735 is to 5346
        therefore 6917 is to ?

Test 3.2   Progressive matrices test

The 10 questions here are designed to test and exercise your appreciation of pattern and design, your ability to think logically but at the same time to explore with an open mind the various possibilities that might lead to a correct solution.

In tests of intelligence, a matrix is an array of squares in which one of the squares has been omitted, and where you must choose the correct missing square from a number of options. It is therefore necessary to study the matrix to decide what pattern is occurring, either by looking across each line and down each column, looking at the array as a whole or looking at the relationship between different squares within the array.

The test that follows consists of 10 questions which gradually increase in difficulty as the test progresses, first starting with 2×2 arrays, then 3×3 arrays and finally 4×4 arrays. The tests also call for a degree of creative thinking, in which you must apply your mind to each set of diagrams in order to appreciate the patterns and sequences that are occurring.

Logical reasoning

You have 45 minutes in which to solve the 10 questions.

1

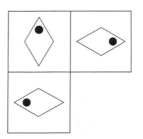

Which is the missing square?

A   B   C   D   E

2

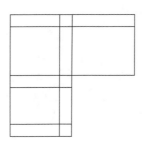

Which is the missing square?

A   B   C   D   E

3

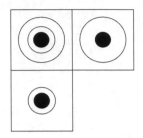

Which is the missing square?

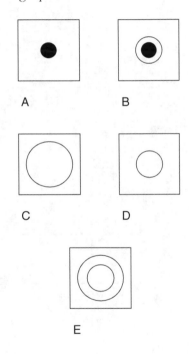

Logical reasoning

4

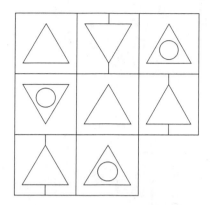

Which is the missing square?

| A | B | C |

| D | E | F |

| G | H |

5

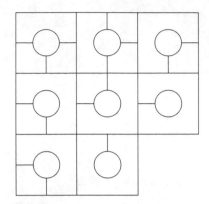

Which is the missing square?

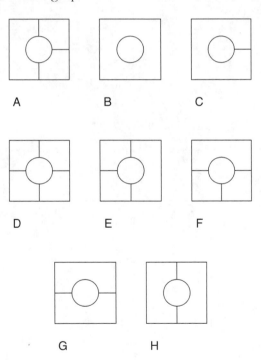

A   B   C

D   E   F

G   H

6

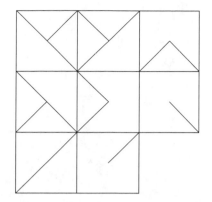

Which is the missing square?

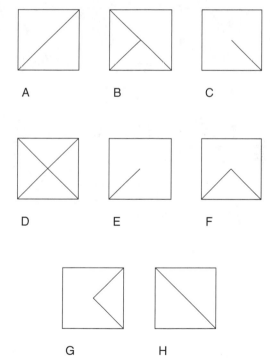

A   B   C

D   E   F

G   H

7

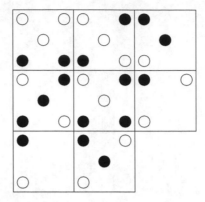

Which is the missing square?

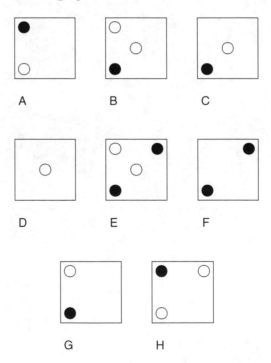

A   B   C

D   E   F

G   H

8

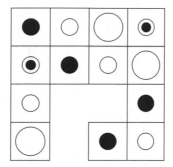

Which is the missing section?

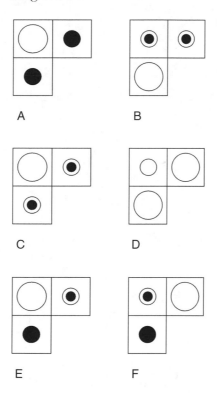

A   B

C   D

E   F

9

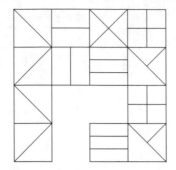

Which is the missing section?

A

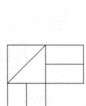

B

C

D

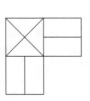

E

F

10

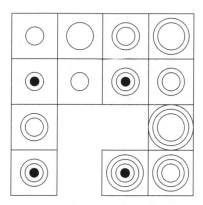

Which is the missing section?

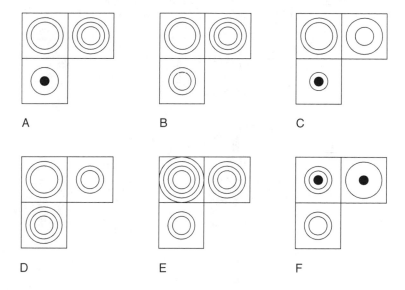

A   B   C

D   E   F

Test 3.3   Advanced logic test

This test is very similar to Test 1 but with a higher degree of difficulty. As in the case of Test 1, there is no specialised knowledge of mathematics or vocabulary required in order to solve these questions, just the ability to think clearly and analytically.

You have 90 minutes in which to solve the 10 questions.

1

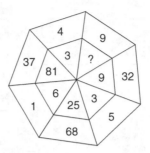

What number should replace the question mark?

2

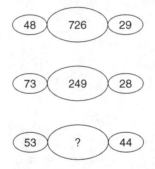

What number should replace the question mark?

3

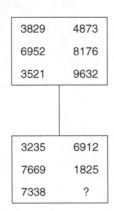

What number should replace the question mark?

4   senate, banana, mirage, curate, revoke

Which one of the words below belongs with the words above?

ginger, humane, abacus, yogurt, sector

5   Five suspects, one of whom is the guilty party, are being
interrogated by the police. Who is the culprit if just three only of
the following statements are correct?

Alf: 'Dave did it.'
Ben: 'It wasn't me.'
Charlie: 'Ernie is innocent.'
Dave: 'Alf is lying when he accuses me.'
Ernie: 'Ben is telling the truth.'

6

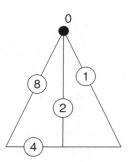

If the number 1943 is represented by the symbols:

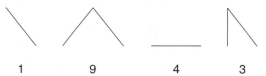

    1   9   4   3

what number is represented by the symbols:

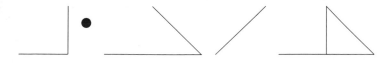

7

5	7	8	6	8	6
8	6	3	?	7	4
2	?	7	8	6	8
5	8	?	4	5	?
3	1	7	2	8	6
7	4	8	5	7	3

What numbers should replace the question marks?

8

A   B   C   D   E

Which is the odd one out?

9 ● Start with a full cup of black coffee (no milk) and drink one-third of it.
   ● Now pour into the cup an amount of milk equal to the coffee you have just drunk, and stir well.
   ● Now drink a further half of the resultant mixture.
   ● Now pour into the cup a further amount of milk equal to the mixture you have just drunk and stir well again.
   ● Now drink one-sixth of the resultant mixture.
   ● Now pour into the cup a further amount of milk equal to the mixture you have just drunk, stir well, and finally, drink the whole cup of liquid.

Have you drunk more milk or more coffee in total?

Logical reasoning

10 ● You have five bags, each containing 10 balls. One bag contains red balls, one bag contains yellow, one bag contains green, one bag contains blue and one bag contains brown.

● All of the balls in four of the bags weigh 20 grams and all the balls in one of the bags, you do not know which bag, weigh 18 grams, i.e. they are 2 grams less than the other balls.

By using a single tray scale (and not a two-tray Libra-type scale), how can you find out in the *minimum* number of weighings which bag contains the lighter balls?

4   Creativity

In the creative state a man is taken out of himself. He lets down
as it were a bucket into his subconscious and draws up something
which is normally beyond his reach. He mixes this thing with
his normal experiences and out of the mixture he makes a work
of art.

E. M. Forster

The term 'creativity' refers to mental processes that lead to solutions,
ideas, concepts, artistic forms, theories or products that are unique or
novel. It has sometimes been referred to as 'the eighth intelligence'.

In this chapter there will be an opportunity not only to explore your
creative talents and potential in general, but also the specific creative
thought processes of imagination, lateral thinking and problem solving.

As a result of work carried out in the 1960s by the American
neurologist Roger Wolcott Sperry (1913–1994), it became apparent
that the creative functions of human beings are controlled by the right-
hand hemisphere of the human brain. This is the side of the brain which
is under-used by the majority of people, as opposed to the thought
processes of the left-hand hemisphere, which is characterised by order,
sequence and logic; and is responsible for such functions as numerical
and verbal skills.

Sperry shared the 1981 Nobel Prize in physiology or medicine
for his split-brain research, which serves as the basis for our current
understanding of cerebral specialisation in the human brain. From the
1960s his work with human patients proved to be of major significance
in the development of neurobiology and psychobiology. He published

his ground-breaking discovery of two separately functioning hemispheres of the brain in 1968.

Thanks to people such as Sperry, in the second half of the twentieth century we have become much more aware of the importance of the human brain, its functioning and its relationship to our body; in fact we have learned more about the brain in the past decade or so than in all of the previous centuries, and one area in which we have obtained a much greater understanding concerns the specialisation of the cerebral hemispheres.

Throughout history it has been accepted that human beings are all different in their own way; in other words, each one of us is an individual with his/her own physical make-up, fingerprints, DNA, facial features, character and personality. These characteristics have always been analysed and categorised, but it was not until the mid-twentieth century that it was realised that each one of us has two sides to his/her brain, each of which have quite different functions and characteristics.

In the 1960s, Roger Sperry, Michael Gazzanniga and Joseph Bogan began a series of ground-breaking experiments that seemed to indicate certain types of thinking were related to certain parts of the brain.

Research, begun in the 1950s, had found that the cerebral cortex has two halves, called hemispheres, which are almost identical. These two brain hemispheres are connected by a bridge, or interface, of millions of nerve fibres called the corpus callosum, which allows them to communicate with each other. The left side of the brain connects to the right side of the body, while the right side of the brain connects to the left side.

In order to work to its full potential, each of these hemispheres must be capable of analysing its own input first, only exchanging information with the other half, by means of the interface, when a considerable amount of processing has taken place.

Because both hemispheres are capable of working independently, human beings are able to process two streams of information at once. The brain then compares and integrates the information to obtain a broader and more in-depth understanding of the concept under examination.

In the early 1960s, Sperry and his team showed by a series of experiments, first using animals whose corpus callosum had been severed, and then on human patients whose corpus callosum had been severed in an attempt to cure epilepsy, that each of the two hemispheres has developed specialised functions and has its own private sensations, perceptions, ideas and thoughts, all separate from the opposite hemisphere.

As their experiments continued, Sperry and his team were able to reveal much more about how the two hemispheres were specialised to perform different tasks. The left side of the brain is analytical and functions in a sequential and logical fashion and is the side which controls language, academic studies and rationality. The right side is creative and intuitive and leads, for example, to the birth of ideas for works of art and music.

The contrasting right- and left-hemisphere functions, sometimes referred to as '*laterality*', can be summarised as follows:

Left hemisphere	Right hemisphere
Parsing	Holistic
Logic	Intuition
Conscious thought	Subconscious thought
Outer awareness	Inner awareness
Methods, rules	Creativity
Written language	Insight
Number skills	Three-dimensional forms
Reasoning	Imagination
Scientific skills	Music, art
Aggression	Passive
Sequential	Simultaneous
Verbal intelligence	Practical intelligence
Intellectual	Sensuous
Analytical	Synthetic

The meaning of the word 'lateral' is *of or relating to the side, away from the median axis*. The term 'laterality' – or 'sidedness' – is used to refer to any one of a number of preferences for one side of the body to another. Probably the most common example of this, and one to which we can all relate, is whether a person is left- or right-handed. In recent years the term 'laterality' has come to be used very much to characterise the asymmetry of the hemispheres of the brain with regard to specific cognitive functions, as demonstrated by the list above.

While some individuals may be heavily weighted towards a particular hemisphere, this does not mean they are predominant in every one of that particular hemisphere's skills, since no-one is entirely left- or right-brained, e.g. while some individuals may have a strong overall bias towards left-side brain dominance, it may be that they still under-perform on, for instance numerical tests, and therefore need to work at that particular skill.

There is also always going to be an overlap between certain brain functions of opposing hemispheres, e.g. functions using logical processes and lateral thinking processes, where one is a predominantly right-brain function and the other is a predominantly left-brain function. However, when logical processes are being used, the right brain does not switch off and vice versa. On the contrary, both of these brain processes work much more effectively when both sides of the brain are working together.

The importance to each of us of accessing both hemispheres of the brain is considerable. In order to support the whole brain function, logic and intuition, to give just two examples, are equally important. Before the subconscious of the right-hand hemisphere can function, it needs the fuel, or data, that has been fed into, collated and processed by the left-hand hemisphere. One danger is the overburdening of the left-hand hemisphere with too much data, and too quickly, to the extent that the creative side of the brain is unable to function to its full potential. On the other hand, lack of data fed into the left-hand hemisphere could result in the creative side, or right hemisphere, 'drying up'. It is therefore desirable to strike the right balance between right and left hemispheres in order for the brain to work to its full potential.

Because it is under-used, much creative talent in many people remains untapped throughout life. Until we try, most of us never know what we can actually achieve. We all have a creative side to our brain, therefore we should all have the potential to be creative. However, because of the pressures of modern living and the need for specialisation in order to develop a successful career, many of us never have the time or opportunity, or indeed are never given the encouragement, to explore our latent talents, even though most of us have sufficient ammunition to realise this potential in the form of data which has been fed into, collated and processed by the brain during our lifetime.

Like many other tasks, or pleasures, we never know what we can achieve until we try. Having then tried, we instinctively know whether we find it enjoyable or whether we have a talent or flair for it. Then, if these signs are positive, we must persevere. By cultivating new leisure activities and pursuing new pastimes, it is possible for each of us to explore the potential and often vastly under-used parts of the human brain.

Test 4.0 Creativity personality test

In each of the following, choose from a scale of 1–5 which of these statements you most agree with or is most applicable to yourself. Choose just one of the numbers 1–5 in each of the 25 statements. Choose 5 for most agree/most applicable option, down to 1 for least agree/least applicable:

1 I find it very difficult to concentrate on just one subject or project for a long period without breaking off to do other things.

    5   4   3   2   1

2 I am more of a visionary, rather than someone who is down to earth and businesslike.

    5   4   3   2   1

3 I often have the urge to try out a new hobby, such as painting or playing a musical instrument.

    5   4   3   2   1

Creativity

4 I am not afraid to voice unpopular opinions.

    5   4   3   2   1

5 I like to retire into my own thoughts uninterrupted for a thinking session.

    5   4   3   2   1

6 I would describe myself as more disordered than methodical.

    5   4   3   2   1

7 The greatest teacher of all is experience.

    5   4   3   2   1

8 I am more sensitive than the average person when it comes to environmental issues.

    5   4   3   2   1

9 I have more of an interest and/or curiosity in modern art than a 'dismissing it as rubbish' attitude.

    5   4   3   2   1

10 I often have the urge to take things apart to see how they work.

    5   4   3   2   1

11 I have a very overactive mind, to the extent that I sometimes find it difficult to get to sleep at night.

    5   4   3   2   1

12 I enjoy being unconventional.

    5   4   3   2   1

13 I am more of an intuitive person than an intellectual.

     5   4   3   2   1

14 When attending a talk or lecture, I often find myself drifting off and thinking of other things.

     5   4   3   2   1

15 I sometimes get very frustrated with myself if I cannot do something as well as I would like to.

     5   4   3   2   1

16 I prefer solitude and scenery to lively social gatherings.

     5   4   3   2   1

17 I often find myself irritated by petty rules and regulations.

     5   4   3   2   1

18 I have a very lively imagination.

     5   4   3   2   1

19 I am often very impatient to learn new things.

     5   4   3   2   1

20 I more than occasionally have dreams that I am unable to explain.

     5   4   3   2   1

21 I am very independent minded.

     5   4   3   2   1

22 Anytime I get a flash of inspiration or a new idea, my mind cannot rest until I have tried to put it into practice.

5   4   3   2   1

23 I enjoy spending time on my own.

5   4   3   2   1

24 I revel in being different to others.

5   4   3   2   1

25 When hanging onto the phone, with a pencil in my hand and a piece of paper in front of me, the probability is that I will start to doodle.

5   4   3   2   1

Section I – Imagination

> Imagination is more important than knowledge. For while knowledge defines all we currently know and understand, imagination points to all we might discover and create.
>
> Albert Einstein

Imagination is the process of recombining memories of past experiences and images into novel constructions. Thus, imagination is both creative and constructive, it can be either wishful or realistic, involve future plans, or be merely a mental review of the past.

Imagination, perception and memory are essentially similar mental processes and can each be defined as follows:

Imagination – the conscious mental process of invoking ideas or images of objects and events.

Perception – the conscious integration of sensory impressions of external objects and events, including how we perceive others and how others perceive us. It also envelopes how we perceive the world as a whole – the big picture – and how we perceive different scenarios and situations that appear within the big picture.

Memory (the 'ninth intelligence') – the mental evocation of past experiences.

One important aspect of perception is the ability to see more than one point of view. If, for example, you look at the two drawings below, at first glance what you see appears to be quite unambiguous:

However, if you continue to stare at each figure in turn, and keep your attention on it focused, then the orientation suddenly shifts and you find yourself looking at a quite different figure from what you first imagined.

These two figures, therefore, illustrate the importance of perception. Two different viewpoints appear – yet they are both correct. If anything, this teaches us that we should endeavour to see both viewpoints, and both sides of an argument.

Now look at the figure below. What do you see?

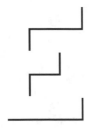

Creativity

Most people will say that the figure is the letter E. If, however, they look closely they will see that there is no letter E, just three sets of lines. It is because our mind is conditioned to what it believes it wants to see, i.e. the image of the most common letter of the alphabet, which it has seen many thousands of times, that it completes the object for you and makes you come to the conclusion that you perceive something that in reality does not exist.

Now read the following paragraph:

I cdnuolt blveiee taht I cluod aulaclty uesdnatnrd waht I was rdgnieg. The phaonmneal pweor of the hmuan mnid Aoccdrnig to a rscheearch at Cmabrigde Uinervtisy, it deosn't mttaer in waht oredr the ltteers in a wrod are, The olny iprmoatnt tihng is taht the frist and lsat ltteer be in the rghit pclae. The rset can be a taotl mses and you can sitll raed it wouthit a porbelm. Tihs is bcuseae the huamn mnid deos not raed ervey lteter by istlef, but the wrod as a wlohe.

Again, our mind has taken over. It knows from past experience what it wants to see, and as a result the task of reading what, at first, appears be a load of mumbo-jumbo is surprisingly easy.

The following tests are all designed to test your powers of imagination and creativity.

Test 4.1   Imaginative shapes

In each of the following, use your imagination to create an original sketch or drawing of something recognisable incorporating the lines already provided:

You have 30 minutes in which to complete the nine drawings.

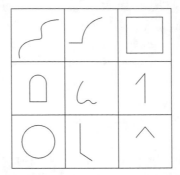

Test 4.2   Wild imagination

The object of this test is to interpret each of the 20 drawings in the wildest and most imaginative way you can. You may also try playing the game with other people. The wilder someone's suggestion is, the better it is and the more creative they are. Let your imagination run riot and see what you can come up with.

This test is not timed or marked as it is simply an exercise in creative thinking.

Creativity

Test 4.3   Creative logic

These questions require some logic, together with a high degree of spatial awareness and creative thinking, and flexibility of mind in adapting to different types of questions.

You have 30 minutes in which to complete the 10 questions.

1 Which is the odd one out?

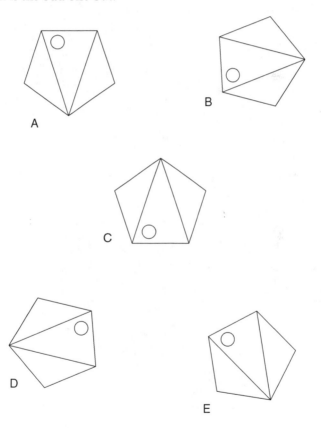

2

To which hexagon below can a dot be added so that it then meets the same conditions as in the hexagon above?

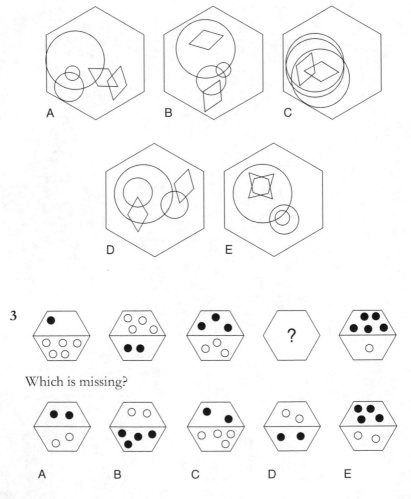

A

B

C

D

E

3

Which is missing?

A   B   C   D   E

4

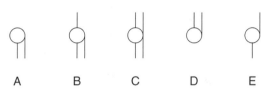

What comes next?

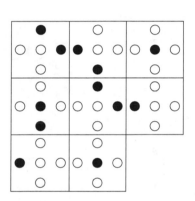

A   B   C   D   E

5

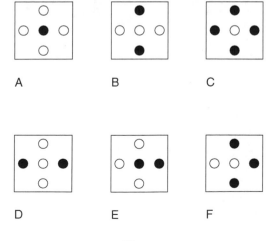

Which is the missing tile?

A   B   C

D   E   F

6

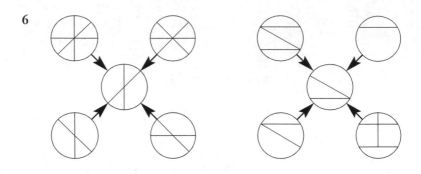

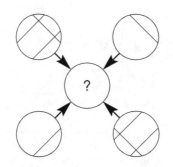

Which circle should replace the question mark?

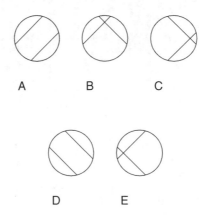

A   B   C

D   E

Creativity

7 Which is the odd one out?

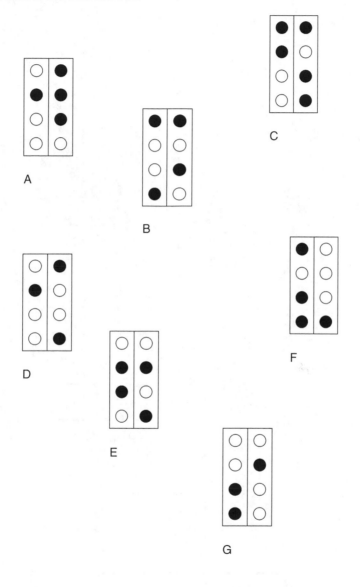

A

B

C

D

E

F

G

8 Which is the odd one out?

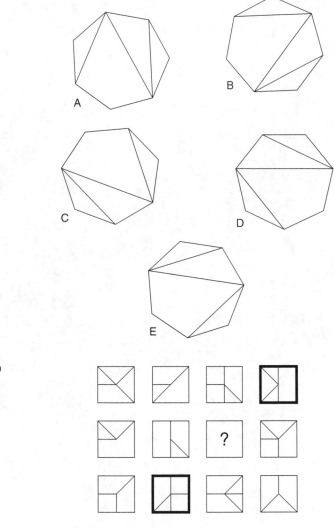

9

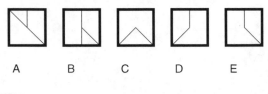

Which square should replace the question mark?

A   B   C   D   E

10 Which is the odd one out?

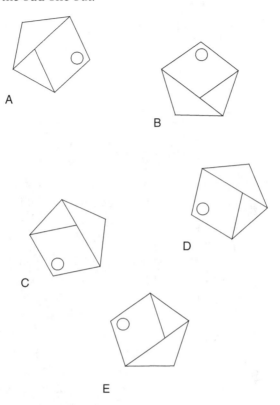

A

B

C

D

E

Test 4.4   The bucket test

The following test is based on Gestalt and Jackson's test of divergent ability, which requires the subject to name as many new uses as possible for an object such as a comb or a paper clip.

In this test you are required to name as many uses as possible for a bucket.

Allow yourself 6 minutes to write up to 10 suggestions.

————————————————

————————————————

————————————————

———————————————
———————————————
———————————————
———————————————
———————————————
———————————————
———————————————

Section II – Lateral thinking

The term 'lateral thinking' was originated by its creator and pioneer, Dr Edward de Bono, and is a systematic way of approaching creative thinking.

The word 'lateral' means *of or relating to either side, away from the median axis*. Lateral thinking is a method of seeking to solve problems by unique and different ways, by attempting to look at that problem from many angles rather than searching for a direct head-on solution.

It therefore involves the need to think outside the box and develop a degree of creative, innovative thinking, which seeks to change our natural and traditional perceptions, concepts and ideas. By developing this type of thinking, we greatly increase our ability to solve problems facing us that we could not otherwise solve.

To solve all the questions that appear in this section, it is necessary to think laterally and creatively and to look for solutions that may not seem apparent on first inspection.

Test 4.5   Lateral thinking test

This test consists of 10 puzzles, all designed to exercise powers of lateral thinking and encourage creative thought in seeking out sometimes unexpected solutions.

For those readers wishing to assess their performance against the clock, there is a time limit of 90 minutes allowed for completing all 10 questions.

Creativity

If, however, you prefer simply to dip into these questions at random and attempt which ever one takes your fancy at the time, it is suggested that, if you do not find a solution immediately, you do not rush to look up the answer but instead return to the question sometime later, as a puzzle that may baffle you at first may become soluble when you take a fresh look. It is possible that your mind has been subconsciously working on the problem and that the answer which previously eluded you may suddenly become apparent.

1
R	N	Y		D	E	P		N	D	?
A	E	R		E	V	O		A	I	?
C	P	T		R	E	L		C	D	?

What letters should replace the question marks?

2 onerously, honeymoon, pioneered, wagonette

What word below continues the above sequence?

prisoners, aborigine, cautioned, erroneous, astronomy

(*Hint: page 205*)

3

1	0	7
2	3	6
3	4	3
5	7	9
?	?	?

What numbers should replace the question marks?

4

N	T
P	R

G	I
K	M

F	H
?	L

What letter should replace the question mark?

5

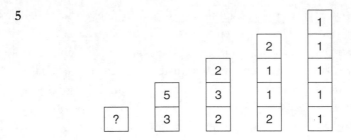

What number should replace the question mark?

6

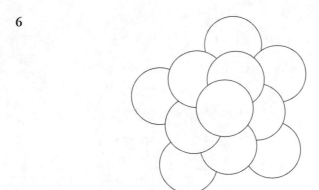

How many circles appear above?

7

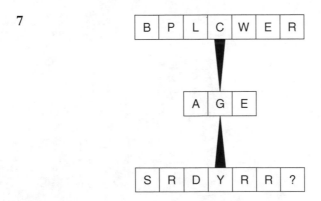

What letter should replace the question mark?

8

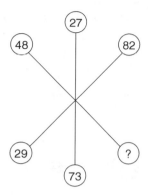

What number should replace the question mark?

9

What letter should replace the question mark?

10 WAVE = 13
TAXI = 8
HALT = 10
FAIL = ?
LINK = 9

What value is FAIL?

Test 4.6   Lateral thinking exercises

The puzzles in this test are not timed and an assessment is not provided. They are included purely and simply in order to exercise powers of lateral thinking and encourage creative thought.

It is suggested that should you not find a solution immediately, you do not rush to look up the answer but instead return to the question some time later. It may be that your mind has been subconsciously working on the problem and that an answer which previously may have eluded you may suddenly become apparent.

1

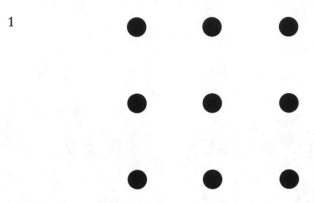

Join all nine dots with four straight lines without taking your pencil off the paper.

2 ENEI = 78
   URON = 41
   NESE = 97
   ???? = 86

   (Hint: page 205)

3

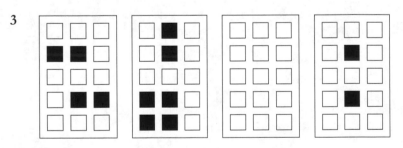

Which windows in the third figure should be blacked out?

   (Hint: page 205)

4 What is it that when you remove the whole you still have some left?

5

      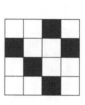

1   2   3

   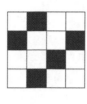   

4   5   6

Which is the odd one out?

(*Hint: page 205*)

6

Reposition two only (no more, no less) of the sticks, so that you end up with four squares of equal size and no sticks left over.

7

Add three sticks to form three squares without disturbing any of the other sticks.

(*Hint: page 205*)

8 A man is working on the edge of the roof perimeter at the very top of the Empire State Building in New York. He slips and falls off the ledge he is working on and falls onto the concrete below. He only suffers very mild concussion and a sprained wrist. Why?

9

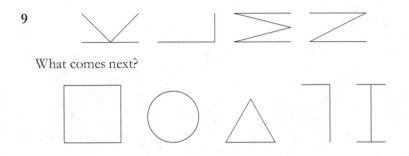

What comes next?

10   sunflower, among, statuette, Sweden, enthusiasm, befriend, ?

What completes the above list?

abbreviated, Denmark, hopelessness, insatiable, criminal

(*Hint: page 205*)

Section III – Problem solving

In psychology, a 'problem' is defined as a situation in which some of the components are already known and additional components must then be ascertained or determined, and 'problem solving' is broadly all the processes involved in the solution of that problem.

There are several problem-solving techniques which have been put into practice over the years, such as brainstorming, critical path analysis and SWOT (strengths, weaknesses, opportunities, threats), which in their own way have often proved successful.

In *brainstorming* techniques, for example, the object is for groups or individuals to break away from conventional and habitual ways of thinking and to generate fresh ideas, which can then be evaluated and the most effective ways selected. Brainstorming is therefore a method of searching for, and developing, creative solutions to a problem by

Creativity

focusing on the problem and deliberately encouraging the participants to come up with as many unusual and creative solutions as possible.

The French mathematicians Poincaré and Hadamard defined the following four stages of creativity:

1. *Preparation*: The attempt to solve a problem by normal means.
2. *Incubation*: When you feel frustrated that the above methods have not worked and as a result you move away to other things.
3. *Illumination*: Eureka!! The answer suddenly comes to you in a flash via your subconscious.
4. *Verification*: Your reasoning powers take over as you analyse the answer which has come to you and assess its feasibility.

Of course, there are other problems which can be solved by using what is often referred to as 'common sense'. Common sense is the almost forgotten tenth type of intelligence, and can hold the key to solving many real-life problems. Take, for instance, the following scenario:

A motorist encounters a shepherd and his dog with a flock of sheep travelling in the same direction on a narrow lane, and finds there is no room to drive through. The shepherd regards the motorist as a nuisance and wants rid of him, as the dog is barking and the sheep are disturbed, and the motorist regards the sheep as a nuisance because he cannot continue his journey. How is the situation resolved amicably to the satisfaction of both the motorist and the shepherd?

You may be forgiven for thinking there appears to be no easy way of solving this problem. However, this need not be the case with the application of a degree of common sense. Consider, therefore, the following solution which was reached to the entire satisfaction of both parties and with the very minimum of inconvenience:

The car stops and the shepherd and his dog drive the sheep back along the lane for a few yards past the car. When all the sheep and the dog are to the rear of the car, the way is then clear for the motorist to continue his journey, and the shepherd is also free to continue his journey unhindered.

Test 4.7 Problem-solving exercises

The puzzles in this section are not timed and an assessment is not provided. They are included purely as problem-solving exercises in finding creative solutions.

As in the case of similar tests in this book, it is suggested that, should you not find a solution immediately, you do not rush to look up the answer but instead return to the question some time later; perhaps even on several occasions.

1

How do you accurately weigh a small puppy with just a standard household step-on weigh scale if the puppy is extremely lively and will not keep still?

2 Many hundreds of years ago a thief was charged with treason against a Roman emperor and sentenced to death. The emperor, feeling slightly merciful, asked the man how he would like to die. Which way would you choose to die if you found yourself in the same situation?

3

Move the position of four sticks only to produce three equilateral triangles.

4 Today Amy celebrates her birthday. Two days later her twin brother Matthew celebrates his birthday. How can this be so?

5

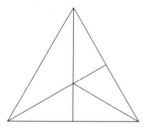

How many triangles appear above? What is the best strategy to adopt when tackling this and similar, but more complicated, triangle-counting puzzles?

6

The sticks produce an equation that is obviously incorrect. Remove three sticks without disturbing the sticks already placed in order to make the equation correct.

7

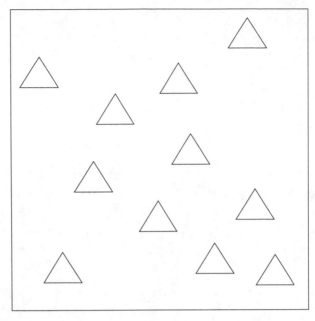

Add the largest possible equilateral triangle so that it does not touch any of the other triangles and does not overlap the side of the rectangle.

(Hint: page 205)

8

Find a way to add 16 sticks, without disturbing any of the 18 already in place, in order to make the equation read correctly.

Creativity

9 Before crowds of people at the arena, the emperor offers the gladiator one last chance to escape death by drawing one of two slips of paper from a bag. The emperor announces that on one piece of paper is written the word 'death' and on the other is written the word 'freedom'. The gladiator's lover, who is the emperor's wife, manages to whisper that both pieces of paper say 'death'. Despite this, the gladiator still wins his freedom. How?

10

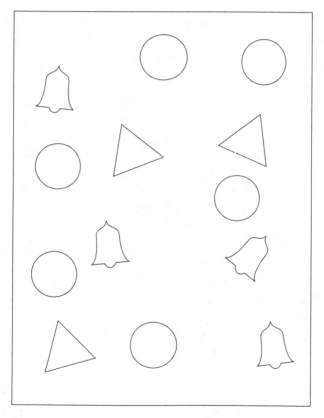

Divide the rectangle into the smallest possible number of segments of equal size and area, so that each segment contains the same number of triangles, bells and circles.

(**Hint: page 205**)

5 Emotional Intelligence

Emotional intelligence, more commonly referred to as emotional quotient (EQ), is the ability to be aware of, control and manage one's own emotions and those of other people. The two main aspects of EQ are:

- Understanding yourself, your goals, aspirations, responses and behaviour.
- Understanding others and their feelings.

The concept of emotional intelligence was developed in the mid-1990s by Daniel Goldman, coming to prominence with his 1995 book *Emotional Intelligence*. The early emotional intelligence theory was originally developed in the USA during the 1970s and 1980s by the work and writings of Howard Gardner of Harvard University, Peter Salovy (Yale) and John Mayer (New Hampshire).

The EQ concept argues that IQ, which has tended to be the traditional measure of intelligence, is too narrow and that there are wider areas of emotional intelligence, such as behavioural and character elements, that help to dictate how successful we are. It is because of this that emotional intelligence, in addition to aptitude testing, is now an important part of recruitment interviewing and selection procedures.

Although scoring highly in an aptitude test may impress a prospective employer, it does not reveal the full story, as it does not automatically follow that the applicant will be suited to the position for which they are applying. While they may be intellectually qualified to do the actual job, it may be they do not actually enjoy many aspects of the work involved or will not fit into a team, as a result of which they would be very likely to under-perform.

To prevent such a mismatch occurring, personality profiling tests are becoming increasingly common as part of the job interview process. Such tests measure personality traits, e.g. how you relate to other people; how you relate to emotions, both your own and those of your colleagues; how you respond to stressful situations; or what motivates you.

In general, the term 'personality' refers to the patterns of thought, feeling and behaviour that are unique in every one of us, and these are the characteristics that distinguish us from other people. Our personality thus implies the predictability of how we are likely to act or react under different circumstances, although in reality nothing is quite that simple and our reactions to situations are never entirely predictable.

Goldman summarized the five EQ domains as:

1. Knowing your emotions.
2. Managing your emotions.
3. Motivating yourself.
4. Recognising and understanding other people's emotions.
5. Managing relationships, i.e. managing the emotions of others.

It is now widely recognised that if someone is deemed intellectually intelligent, it does not necessarily follow they are also emotionally intelligent, and possessing a high IQ rating does not mean that success will automatically follow.

Being intellectually brilliant does not mean that persons are able to relate to other people socially, neither does it mean they are capable of managing their own emotions or able to motivate themselves.

The following questionnaires are designed to test different aspects of your personality. The procedure for completing each of these is to answer the questions as truthfully and as realistically as possible; in other words, be true to yourself at all times in order to obtain the most accurate assessment.

There is no need to read through these tests first before attempting them: just answer intuitively and without too much consideration. There are no right or wrong answers and, although you should work as quickly as possible, there is no set time limit.

Test 5.1   Anxious or relaxed

In each of the following choose from a scale of 1–5 which of these statements you most agree with or is most applicable to yourself. Choose just one of the numbers 1–5 in each of the 25 statements. Choose 5 for most agree/most applicable, down to 1 for least agree/least applicable.

1 I often have to work to tight deadlines.

<blockquote>

5   4   3   2   1

</blockquote>

2 Loud noise aggravates me.

<blockquote>

5   4   3   2   1

</blockquote>

3 When I get little aches and pains, I often worry that it could be something more serious.

<blockquote>

5   4   3   2   1

</blockquote>

4 Sometimes I cannot get to sleep as I have too much on my mind.

<blockquote>

5   4   3   2   1

</blockquote>

5 I find it difficult to switch off completely and totally relax.

<blockquote>

5   4   3   2   1

</blockquote>

6 I sometimes get angry with myself if I make a mistake or do not do something to the standard I have set myself.

<blockquote>

5   4   3   2   1

</blockquote>

7 I often find myself dashing around at more than my normal speed.

<blockquote>

5   4   3   2   1

</blockquote>

8 I feel ruled by time.

    5   4   3   2   1

9 I am a fast talker.

    5   4   3   2   1

10 I easily become agitated in queues and traffic jams.

    5   4   3   2   1

11 I am often critical of others.

    5   4   3   2   1

12 I do not suffer fools gladly.

    5   4   3   2   1

13 I push myself hard.

    5   4   3   2   1

14 I am much more of a serious person than a jovial one.

    5   4   3   2   1

15 I tend to gesticulate a lot.

    5   4   3   2   1

16 Punctuality is important to me.

    5   4   3   2   1

17 There has on several different occasions in my life been just one particular thing which has dominated my thoughts for days on end.

    5   4   3   2   1

18 It is important to me that I play to win.

   5   4   3   2   1

19 I have on several occasions gone red in the face with harassment.

   5   4   '3   2   1

20 I am a worrier.

   5   4   3   2   1

21 I am not optimistic about the future.

   5   4   3   2   1

22 I worry that I am not more financially secure.

   5   4   3   2   1

23 I am impatient.

   5   4   3   2   1

24 I want people to see me as one of life's winners.

   5   4   3   2   1

25 I often wake up in the morning with something worrying on my mind.

   5   4   3   2   1

Assessment

Total score 90–125

Your score indicates that you are of a somewhat overly anxious nature who finds it very difficult to relax completely, and you are constantly on your toes for any unforeseen event that may occur. You also have the tendency to build many things up in your own mind out of all proportion.

As this is in your nature and possibly the way by which you deal with things and cope with pressure, it is nevertheless important to try and adopt a more relaxed attitude to life, since anxiety does lead to stress and stress is the cause of many serious health problems.

It is necessary sometimes for overly anxious people to make a concerted effort to relax more, and one way of doing this may be by cultivating new interests and by taking one step back and reflecting on their life and its positive aspects.

In times of extreme anxiety, it may be necessary to try and temporarily switch off completely from your daily routine and try to relax and chill out completely for a few days by doing something you really enjoy, whether it be lazing around the garden, listening to music, having a few rounds of golf or spending quality time with friends and family. This may well enable you to get things into perspective and help you cultivate a more relaxed attitude to life.

It is also important to all of us, but especially overly anxious people, that we are able to recognise any early warning signs that we are pushing ourselves too far. Then we can try to do something about it before it is too late.

Total score 65–89

You are in the fortunate position that although, like all people, you find yourself stressed out to a certain degree from time to time, this tends to be the exception rather than the rule. Anxiety for you is no more of a problem than it is for the average person.

Generally you appear to be a well-balanced person who is able to face up to problems as they arise and does not spend too much time worrying about things that may never happen. You also appear to have sufficient resolve to face up to any stressful situations that may occur in the future.

You are able to recognise any early warning signs that you may be pushing yourself too hard and, on these occasions, are able to do something about this by switching off somewhat and slowing down a little.

Total score less than 65

Whilst you do worry on occasions, as do all of us, you appear to have a laid-back, relaxed attitude to life, with the result that high anxiety is less of a problem for you than it is for the average person.

This attitude can have a calming influence, not just on yourself but also on those around you.

One word of caution to having an almost totally relaxed attitude to life is believing that problems will never occur. We all have to face up to numerous problems in our lifetime. Often, if we are able to anticipate such problems, we are able to minimise or even avoid them. Consequently, on occasions, a degree of forward planning is desirable. You should therefore have the ability to plan ahead and also build in a leeway for the unexpected.

It is also worth bearing in mind that a certain amount of tension is positive. People often respond to, and are encouraged by, challenges.

Test 5.2   Extrovert or introvert

Answer each question or statement by choosing which one of the three alternative responses given is most applicable to you.

1 Do you prefer to work alone, or as part of a team?

   a)   No strong preference.
   b)   Alone.
   c)   As part of a team.

2 How much do you enjoy social gatherings?

   a)   I can take them or leave them.
   b)   Very little.
   c)   Very much.

3 What is your ideal way of celebrating your birthday?

   a) Going out for a meal with a few family or friends.
   b) I prefer my birthday to be just like any other normal day.
   c) A surprise party with lots of family and friends.

4 Are you more comfortable when talking to people on a one-to-one basis or in a group discussion?

   a) No strong preference.
   b) On a one-to-one basis.
   c) In a group discussion.

5 How quickly do you become bored and restless when performing routine tasks?

   a) Fairly quickly.
   b) Not very quickly, as I am able to apply my mind to, and concentrate on, the task in hand.
   c) Extremely quickly.

6 When travelling alone on a long train journey would you be likely to strike up a long conversation with a complete stranger sitting next to you?

   a) Maybe not a long conversation but I might exchange a few pleasantries with them.
   b) Not really.
   c) Yes I would really enjoy having a lengthy conversation with them.

7 How often do you like to let your hair down, let yourself go and have a real good time?

   a) Just occasionally.
   b) Hardly ever at all, as that is not really my idea of enjoyment.
   c) As often as possible.

8 If you were asked to give a speech at a function, would you feel happy about doing this?

    a) It wouldn't worry me, although I may be a little nervous beforehand.

    b) No, as I would be very nervous.

    c) Yes, I would relish the prospect.

9 How easily do you make friends?

    a) Fairly easily.

    b) Not easily.

    c) Very easily.

10 If you need to approach someone in high authority for a favour, would you prefer to ask them:

    a) By telephone.

    b) By letter or email.

    c) Face to face.

11 How quickly are you on the dance floor at a social function?

    a) I tend to go with the flow and join in more or less at the same time as everyone else.

    b) I don't venture on the dance floor if I can avoid it.

    c) Usually one of the first.

12 Would you describe yourself as a leader or a follower?

    a) A bit of both, depending on the situation or circumstances.

    b) Generally a follower.

    c) Generally a leader.

13 What would be your reaction if someone asked you to sell some raffle tickets for charity?

a) I would probably accept, but say that I might not be able to sell them all.
b) I would probably have to decline, as I would be unlikely to sell them.
c) I would accept, and would not expect to have any problem selling the tickets.

14 Do you think people see you as a fun person?

a) Perhaps, in certain ways.
b) I doubt it.
c) Hopefully.

15 What would be your reaction if the position of chair suddenly became vacant on a committee on which you were sitting?

a) I may consider the position of chairperson, but only if approached by one of the other committee members to stand for election.
b) I would not wish to become the next chairperson.
c) I would probably push to become the next chairperson.

16 How often do you let your opinions be known?

a) Whenever I feel it is necessary.
b) Only when pressed to do so.
c) Frequently.

17 Do you enjoy being the centre of attention?

a) Perhaps so, occasionally.
b) No.
c) Yes.

18 Which of the following words would you say is the most applicable to you?

    a)   Tenacious.
    b)   Cautious.
    c)   Popular.

19 Do you enjoy making small talk at buffet lunches?

    a)   It's OK.
    b)   No, I hate small talk and can never think of anything to say.
    c)   Yes, I am quite comfortable when making small talk.

20 Do you prefer to discuss things face-to-face or over the telephone?

    a)   No preference.
    b)   Over the telephone.
    c)   Face-to-face.

21 Would you go out of your way to meet 'the right people'?

    a)   Maybe.
    b)   No.
    c)   Yes.

22 Which of the following words would you say is the most applicable to you?

    a)   Balanced.
    b)   Shy.
    c)   Effervescent.

23 Do you enjoy performing your party piece at Christmas parties and other occasions?

a) Not particularly, but I will join in the fun rather than be seen as a party pooper.
b) No, in any case I don't have a party piece that I could perform.
c) Yes.

24 Would you appear naked on a charity calendar?

a) I would like to think so, but I'm not sure I could pluck up the courage.
b) No way.
c) Yes.

25 Do you ever run out of things to say when talking to someone you have just met?

a) Not usually.
b) Yes, I do sometimes tend to dry up after a while.
c) No, I cannot say that I do, as there is always lots to ask people.

Assessment

Award yourself 2 points for every (c) answer, 1 point for every (a) and 0 points for every (b).

40–50 points

Your score indicates that you are an extrovert who enjoys being the centre of attention and cannot by any stretch of the imagination be called a shrinking violet.

This generally means that you will not be lacking in outer confidence and you will always appear to be trying to get the most out of life, although it is possible that some people who give the impression of being extroverts are acting in this way in order to cover up their inner self-doubts and anxieties.

Although many people will admire your zest and energy, you should nevertheless take care not to be too much of an extrovert to the point that people find you excessively pushy, even to the extent of being overbearing. Often someone with a bubbly personality will achieve greater success and win more friends if that personality is tempered with a degree of modesty and sensitivity towards others.

25–39 points

Your score indicates that you are no more of an extrovert or an introvert than the average person.

Although you sometimes may wish that you could be as outgoing as those who appear more extrovert than yourself, it may be that by having the ability to show reserve, especially when it is appropriate, you are probably regarded by other people as someone who they feel relaxed about having in their company.

If, at times, you feel that you are a little shy and 'backward at coming forward', it may be that you secretly admire the way people who are more extrovert than you behave. It is, however, these people who are in the minority and, in fact, you are probably regarded by other people as a person who does possess a much more appealing personality.

Less than 25 points

Although your score indicates that you are quite introverted, this does not mean that you cannot be successful in life.

Many people are extremely modest and shy, but at the same time have the ability to be high achievers in their own field, providing they can recognise their own talents and gain an extra bit of self-confidence to harness their potential.

Although you may prefer to keep your views to yourself, on those occasions where you are bursting to express an opinion, or join in a conversation, you may be afraid of doing so because you worry about what people think, especially if there are a number of people present.

This may be indicative of a lack of confidence in how people will react to you, even to the extent of a feeling of inferiority.

It may be that you do not lack the inner self-confidence and belief in yourself, but are afraid of expressing this inner self in public. You should, however, make a concerted effort to try and gain that extra degree of self-confidence to harness your potential even more and try not to be backward at coming forward.

Test 5.3 Optimist or pessimist

In each of the following, choose from a scale of 1−5 which of these statements you most agree with or is most applicable to yourself. Choose just one of the numbers 1−5 in each of the 25 statements. Choose 5 for most agree/most applicable, down to 1 for least agree/least applicable.

1 I believe that superstitious beliefs, e.g. 'breaking a mirror brings 7 years' bad luck', are bunkum.

   5   4   3   2   1

2 I never even notice the fire regulations when staying in a hotel, let alone read them.

   5   4   3   2   1

3 I believe in keeping my aspirations high at all times.

   5   4   3   2   1

4 You must speculate to accumulate.

   5   4   3   2   1

5 When one door closes another one always opens.

   5   4   3   2   1

6 I never lose sleep through worrying.

5   4   3   2   1

7 I am constantly on the lookout for opportunities to move on to new and exciting ventures.

5   4   3   2   1

8 In life, there is an ideal partner for everyone.

5   4   3   2   1

9 Every dog has his day.

5   4   3   2   1

10 In the long run, things always turn out for the better.

5   4   3   2   1

11 If I lent money to a friend, it would never occur to me that I might not get it back.

5   4   3   2   1

12 I fully expect that one day I will be a big winner on the lottery or premium bonds.

5   4   3   2   1

13 I never worry about my health.

5   4   3   2   1

14 Things are never quite as bad as they appear.

5   4   3   2   1

15 It is a waste of time going to the doctor with minor complaints such as a mild dose of 'flu.

    5   4   3   2   1

16 If at first you don't succeed, you should try, try and try again.

    5   4   3   2   1

17 I rarely or never worry about my financial situation.

    5   4   3   2   1

18 I am always hopeful that the next stroke of good fortune is just around the corner.

    5   4   3   2   1

19 It is always possible to find a silver lining to every cloud if you look hard enough and long enough.

    5   4   3   2   1

20 Ultimately, good will always triumph over evil.

    5   4   3   2   1

21 I look forward to the post arriving in the morning.

    5   4   3   2   1

22 I very rarely carry an umbrella around with me.

    5   4   3   2   1

23 I always look forward to the future with high expectations.

    5   4   3   2   1

24 Something positive always comes from adversity.

    5   4   3   2   1

25 I am all in favour of taking calculated risks.

    5   4   3   2   1

Assessment

Total score 90–125
Mr Micawber was Charles Dickens' eternal optimist, always expecting that something would turn up. Your score indicates that you are a twenty-first century Mr Micawber.

This is a wonderful and enviable outlook on life to possess. You have the ability somehow to look on the bright side whatever happens and firmly believe that for every dark cloud a silver lining will appear, and that for every bad event something positive will emerge.

Provided you do not become naïve or complacent about life's sometimes harsh realities, you will remain largely cheerful and to a great extent carefree, knowing that by adopting this attitude you can get the best out of life, just as long as you are prepared to accept the inevitable downs with the ups.

Total score 65–89
Life is to a great extent a roller coaster, it can be exciting and stimulating, there are high points and there are low points.

Like the majority of people, you cannot be described as either a pessimist or an optimist. Instead you are a realist, but you are hopeful that the high points in life exceed the low points, which they usually do, providing that we do not exaggerate the low points in our own mind, to the exclusion of the high points.

Although you do not appear to be a pessimist, perhaps one lesson to be learned from the eternal optimist is that pessimists, indeed people in general, always seem to worry too much. It is a fact worth bearing in mind that most of the things we worry about in life never happen anyway, so that in the majority of cases we are worrying unduly.

Total score less than 65

Although you might prefer to describe yourself as a realist, your score does suggest that you have a predominantly pessimistic outlook on life.

Unfortunately this does mean that you are probably perceived by others as a somewhat negative person, and that you frequently suffer from a degree of inner turmoil and loss of sleep.

This is possibly your own way of creating a defensive emotional shield against the consequences of what the future may have in store. Then, if the worst happens, you have prepared yourself for it, but if things turn out better than you anticipated you will feel good – until you start to prepare yourself for the next potential catastrophe.

In actual fact, such a pessimistic attitude does not make anything better or worse in the end, and in some cases causes worry that can lead to stress-related illness and make negative things happen which would not otherwise occur.

One strategy to counteract an overriding pessimistic attitude is not to make mountains out of molehills. Instead, try to concentrate on the positive aspects of life and put negative thoughts to the back of your mind.

Unfortunately this is not so easy to achieve, especially if it is not in your nature to do this, but it is worth the effort as you will then start to feel the benefits, both health-wise and by an improved outlook on life in general.

Test 5.4   Self-confidence

Answer each question or statement by choosing which one of the three alternative responses given is most applicable to you.

1 Do you usually feel good about yourself?

   a)   Sometimes.
   b)   Yes, I generally do.
   c)   Not particularly.

2 Would you relish the opportunity to take part in a political debate on television?

   a)   Not relish the opportunity; however, I may take part but would be quite nervous about it.
   b)   Yes, very much so.
   c)   No, the thought sounds rather scary.

3 How much do you feel in control of your own life?

   a)   Only partly in control.
   b)   Very much.
   c)   Not very much.

4 Do you enjoy circulating and meeting new people at social gatherings?

   a)   I don't mind meeting new people but generally stay within my own circle of acquaintances.
   b)   Yes.
   c)   No, I prefer to stay within my own circle of acquaintances.

5 How often do you worry about living up to the standards of others?

   a)   Occasionally.
   b)   Never.
   c)   More than occasionally.

6 Would you be afraid of standing up and making your point of view known at a public meeting?

   a)   Not afraid, but somewhat nervous perhaps.
   b)   No.
   c)   Yes.

7 What is most likely to be your reaction if told there was to be a complete reorganisation at your place of work?

   a)   Somewhat apprehensive.
   b)   If possible I would like to be involved in the reorganisation, and would tend to look on the positive side in case it presented me with a better career opportunity.
   c)   Quite alarmed, as such changes frequently lead to redundancies or adverse changes to job descriptions.

8 Are you able to bounce back quickly after serious adversity?

   a)   Usually, although it depends to a great extent on how serious an adversity.
   b)   Yes, I find that I am usually able to bounce back quickly, even from serious adversity.
   c)   Not really, as it takes quite some time to bounce back from serious adversity.

9 Do you ever feel self-conscious in public places?

   a)   Sometimes.
   b)   Never.
   c)   Often.

10 Do you believe it is fun sometimes to live dangerously?

   a)   Perhaps just occasionally.
   b)   Yes.
   c)   No.

11 When you gamble, what are your expectations of winning?

    a)   I am usually cautiously optimistic.
    b)   I am usually very optimistic.
    c)   I am usually not optimistic.

12 When you are having an argument do you always stick to your guns if you honestly believe that you are correct?

    a)   Usually I stick to my guns, but may terminate the argument with a comment such as, 'We will have to agree to differ'.
    b)   Yes, I relish a debate and would try even harder to get my point across.
    c)   Sometimes I have given up an argument and started to think that I might not be correct after all.

13 How often do you put yourself down?

    a)   Occasionally.
    b)   Rarely or never.
    c)   More than occasionally.

14 Would you feel nervous about meeting someone very influential or famous?

    a)   Somewhat nervous.
    b)   No, in fact I would relish the opportunity.
    c)   Very nervous.

15 How often do you feel sad or depressed about your personal circumstances?

    a)   Occasionally.
    b)   Rarely or never.
    c)   More than occasionally.

16 What is your reaction if someone is being particularly unhelpful and negative?

   a) Persevere quietly with trying to make the person understand what you require.

   b) Express your annoyance to them.

   c) Accept the situation and keep your feelings to yourself.

17 How much confidence do you have in your own decisions?

   a) Fairly confident.

   b) A great deal.

   c) More hopeful than confident that I have made the right decision.

18 Are you backward at coming forward?

   a) Sometimes.

   b) No.

   c) Frequently.

19 Do you believe in the power of positive thinking?

   a) Maybe.

   b) Yes.

   c) It is not something I have ever thought about.

20 What are your views on selling yourself?

   a) Sometimes you have to sell yourself in order to achieve your ambitions.

   b) It is very important to sell yourself well in order to succeed.

   c) It is a necessary evil in today's world that you have to sell yourself, but it is not something I am good at doing.

6

21 Does the prospect of making a speech in front of a large audience worry you?

   a) It would make me more nervous than worried.
   b) I would be no more than slightly nervous.
   c) Yes.

22 How often do you set yourself goals?

   a) Occasionally.
   b) More than occasionally.
   c) Rarely or never, as I believe in taking life as it comes.

23 Which of the following most reflects your attitude to change?

   a) Change is sometimes unavoidable.
   b) I am not afraid of change.
   c) I dislike change, as it is often change for the worst.

24 Which of the following most reflects your attitude to failure?

   a) Try, try and try again.
   b) Failure is a learning experience.
   c) Disappointment.

25 Do you believe that in life it is necessary to conform in order to be accepted?

   a) In certain circumstances it is necessary.
   b) No.
   c) Yes.

Assessment

Award yourself 2 points for every (b) answer, 1 point for every (a) and 0 points for every (c).

40–50 points
High self-confidence factor.

Keywords: presumptuous, extrovert, sure.

25–39 points
Average self-confidence factor.

Keywords: secure, positive, sensible.

Less than 25 points
Below average self-confidence factor.

Keywords: diffident, pessimistic, modest, introverted.

Analysis

A definition of 'self-confidence' is assuredness and self-reliance in one's own abilities.

In order to achieve self-confidence, it is necessary that we take a realistic view of ourselves. As a result of this, some individuals will have total confidence in a certain aspect of their lives, such as sporting prowess, but other aspects in which they do not feel so confident, such as academic achievement. Self-confidence need not, therefore, apply to all respects of a person's lifestyle.

Being self-confident does not, therefore, mean being able to do everything. It does mean, however, that when sometimes their aspirations are not fulfilled, self-confident people continue to adopt a positive attitude, make the best of their situation and keep a sense of reality.

By adopting this attitude, self-confident people have the ability, to a great extent, to take control of their own lives, accept themselves for what they are and stand up for their own rights and aspirations in today's sometimes intimidating world, but at the same time keep these aspirations realistic.

Self-confident people very rarely feel unsure of themselves, and preoccupied with negative self thoughts, or put themselves down. Because of this they are rarely sad, depressed or lonely.

At the same time, because they do not feel the need to conform in order to be accepted, self-confident people are not excessively dependent on others to feel good about themselves. They are willing to risk the disapproval of others because of the confidence they possess.

The following are some strategies that can be adopted, and worked at, for developing a greater degree of self-confidence:

- Learn to self-evaluate and take charge of your own life. Do not focus too much on the unrealistic aspirations or standards of others such as parents. Instead, focus on how you feel about yourself, your lifestyle and your own aspirations.
- Evaluate and emphasise your strengths by focusing on your achievements and the talents you possess.
- Even if you fail, give yourself credit for trying. View any failure as a learning experience and as a way of achieving personal growth. Give yourself credit for everything you try to achieve.
- Do not be afraid of taking calculated risks. Regard risk taking as a chance to grasp new opportunities.
- Never be afraid of change. It is inevitable, so welcome and embrace it.
- There is no such thing as perfection, so accept yourself for what you are. At the same time, balance this with the need to improve.
- Never try to please everyone at the same time. It simply is not possible.

Test 5.5   Tough or tender

In each of the following choose from a scale of 1–5 which of these statements you most agree with or is most applicable to yourself. Choose just one of the numbers 1–5 in each of the 25 statements. Choose 5 for most agree/most applicable, down to 1 for least agree/least applicable.

1 I always seem to find myself rooting for the underdog.

5   4   3   2   1

2 I admire people who are prepared to admit they were wrong.

    5   4   3   2   1

3 I feel great sympathy for street beggars.

    5   4   3   2   1

4 I believe that there is such a thing as love at first sight.

    5   4   3   2   1

5 I always feel some sympathy for celebrities who are having a bad time in the press.

    5   4   3   2   1

6 I am turned off completely by vulgar jokes and sexual innuendo.

    5   4   3   2   1

7 After a serious argument with my partner all I want to do is make up as quickly as possible

    5   4   3   2   1

8 If someone does me a bad turn I don't waste time thinking of revenge.

    5   4   3   2   1

9 My heart rules my head more than my head rules my heart.

    5   4   3   2   1

10 I would put in a good word for a work colleague who I thought deserved my support.

    5   4   3   2   1

11 I detest watching movies that contain excessive violence.

    5   4   3   2   1

12 I feel very sorry for people who always seem to be the butt of other people's jokes.

    5   4   3   2   1

13 I would encourage anyone to talk over their troubles with me.

    5   4   3   2   1

14 I have always ensured that I put aside some quality time to spend with my partner.

    5   4   3   2   1

15 I always buy my partner a card or present on St. Valentine's Day.

    5   4   3   2   1

16 On occasions my eyes have filled up with tears when watching a movie, be it happy or sad.

    5   4   3   2   1

17 I get very upset and emotional when watching news coverage of real-life tragedies on television.

    5   4   3   2   1

18 I would always go out of my way to help someone who is going through an emotional trauma.

    5   4   3   2   1

19 I would find it extremely difficult to tell anyone some real home truths.

    5   4   3   2   1

20 I have never found it difficult to forgive and forget.

  5   4   3   2   1

21 I like stroking cats and/or dogs.

  5   4   3   2   1

22 I find it difficult to say 'No' when asked for a favour.

  5   4   3   2   1

23 I am as supportive of others as I am ambitious for my own aspirations.

  5   4   3   2   1

24 I often feel happy for other people.

  5   4   3   2   1

25 People should be much more concerned about other people.

  5   4   3   2   1

Assessment

Total score 90–125
Your score indicates that you are a very caring person who is deeply touched by the feelings of others and often affected and saddened by news bulletins or personal experiences about the plight of others who are suffering misfortunes and tragedy.

It may also mean that you are extremely tactful and diplomatic, always making sure you go to great lengths not to hurt other people's feelings. As such you are a kind-hearted and caring person who will go out of their way to help others. This does mean that you are liked and respected by those who know you.

It does, however, also mean that you may possibly lack the inner toughness and drive that is sometimes necessary to achieve a high degree of success.

It may also mean that occasionally you could be taken advantage of, especially if you find it very difficult, and sometimes impossible, to say no.

Keywords: caring, sharing, soft-hearted, idealistic, romantic.

Total score 65–89

You appear to be a generally tender-hearted person who would never wish to hurt other people's feelings deliberately.

It may be, however, that there is the need to peel off one or two layers before this soft centre is revealed.

The advantage of this is that you are still tough enough to pursue your ambitions and goals while retaining the loving and caring side of your personality.

In your dealings with other people you can be tactful, but occasionally are unable to stop yourself from speaking a few home truths or saying things you might regret later.

You are, however, in the fortunate position of usually knowing when, and when not, things are better left unsaid, and usually your good judgement in this respect will prove beneficial to the person to whom you are directing your remarks.

Keywords: empathetic, concerned, considerate.

Total score less than 65

While your score does indicate a high degree of toughness, it may be that deep beneath this apparent hard exterior there lies something of a soft centre. With some people their apparently hard exterior is, in fact, something of an act as they do not wish to be perceived as being soft or displaying weakness.

Also, although you do not come over as a romantic or sentimentalist, this does not stop you from having a long and lasting relationship and secure family life, and it does not mean that people who are able to accept you for what you are will not respect you and admire your honesty.

It is, however, not just for yourself, but for those around you, important to always keep in mind the feelings of others and to try to empathise with them.

If you are able to empathise with others and maintain their respect, you appear to have the qualities of inner toughness which is sometimes necessary to achieve a great deal of success in your chosen career or business venture.

Keywords: pragmatic, resilient, resolute.

6   Memory

Memory (the 'ninth intelligence') is the process of storing and retrieving information in the brain. It is this process of memory that is central to our learning and thinking.

Human beings are continually learning throughout their lifetime. Only some of this massive volume information is selected and stored in the brain, and is available for recall later when required. Learning is the acquisition of new knowledge and memory is the retention of this knowledge. The combination of learning and memory, therefore, is the basis of all our knowledge and abilities. It is what enables us to consider the past, exist in the present and plan for the future. Its importance and power should not be underestimated.

Every part of our life relies to some extent on memory and is what enables us to walk, study, relax, communicate and play; in fact whatever function we perform, some sort of memory process is at work.

As previously discussed in earlier chapters of this book, there are many different types of intelligence, and people who have outstanding artistic, creative, sporting or practical prowess can all be highly successful, or occasionally geniuses, in their specific field without having a high measured IQ.

Having a good memory is yet another type of intelligence, and could result in high academic success, due to the ability to memorise facts, despite a lower than average IQ measurement.

While little is known about the physiology of memory storage in the brain, what is known is that memory involves the association of several brain systems working together. It is also accepted that the more we use our memory, the better it becomes. It is, therefore, important

Memory

to stimulate the memory by using it to the utmost, learning new skills and using memory-enhancing techniques.

The tests in this chapter are designed to test your powers of memory and to assist you in improving your memory by developing your powers of concentration and disciplining yourself to fix your mind on the subject being studied.

Test 6.1   Pattern recognition A

Study the diagram below for 5 seconds, then wait for 5 minutes and turn to page 195.

Test 6.2   Word association

This exercise tests your ability to remember pairs of words and form associations.

Study the 12 pairs of words below for 10 minutes and use your imagination to link each pair of words, as shown below, in as many ways as possible. Then turn to page 195.

SAUSAGE	BAGPIPES	SLIPPER
TRACTOR	ARROW	PARROT
BLACKBOARD	POTATO	TELEVISION
PARASOL	COMPUTER	CANDLE
ROBOT	NAIL	CHAIR
MANDOLIN	SNAKE	BALLOON
PIPE	PENCIL	DICTIONARY
BRIDGE	TREE	MOUSTACHE

145

Test 6.3   Verbal dexterity and memory test – anagrams

This test consists of 20 sets of letters. From each set of letters a seven-letter word can be produced.

The test is designed to test and develop both your powers of memory and your verbal dexterity. To solve each anagram, you must first memorise each set of seven letters and then use these seven letters to produce a seven-letter English word.

Example: WOKEDRY = KEYWORD

Look at each set of seven letters in turn for just 5 seconds, then look away and try to solve the anagram within 2 minutes without committing anything to paper.

1 IANBATS

2 PHILDON

3 PAINOUT

4 DIMMARE

5 TALLFEE

6 OURPETS

7 NOBREAD

8 CENTCOP

9 DOEPIES

10 TENRAVE

11 OARPANG

12 SHYAREA

13 METHERO

14 TAILMOP

15 RAGMICE

16 TIEZINC

17 TAUTODE

18 COYOMEN

19 ANULTRA

20 VIAROTA

Test 6.4   Number/shape recognition

Study the figure below for 15 seconds, then turn straight to page 198.

Test 6.5   Pattern recognition B

Study the figure below for 5 seconds. Now wait for 5 minutes and turn to page 200.

Test 6.6   Instructions

Read and memorise these instructions for 3 minutes, then turn immediately to page 201:

Start at four.
Go from four to seven.
Then down.
Then right.
Then up.
Then right.
Then to two.
Then left.
Then up.
Then back to four.

Test 6.7   Pattern recognition C

Study the following for 10 seconds, then wait for 2 minutes and turn to page 202.

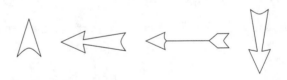

Test 6.8   Shopping list

Study the following shopping list for 5 minutes, then wait for 5 minutes and turn to page 203.

Jar of coffee.
Fish fingers.
Strawberry gateau.
Cheshire cheese.
Tin of baked beans.
Packet of waffles.

Memory

Six rashers of bacon.
Packet of sugar.
French mustard.
Loaf of sliced bread.

Test 6.9   Attention to detail

Study the figure below for 5 minutes, then turn straight to page 203.

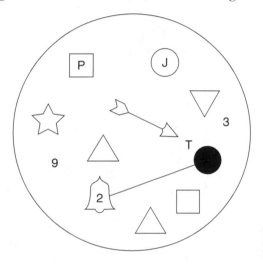

Test 6.10   Memorising an address

Study the address for 2 minutes, then turn to page 204.

David Michael Christiensen
7th Floor
Norwalk House
354 Osprey Drive West
off Threddlethorpe Lane
Netherlee
Keyingham
JU14 9LK

7 Answers, explanations and assessments

Chapter 1 – Introduction

Test 1.1 IQ test

Answers

1 Four stages:

2 1412: $2 + 8 + 4 = 14$; $3 + 9 = 12$

3 arteriole, arthritic, arthritis, arthropod, artichoke, articular, artificer, artillery

4 realistic, impracticable

5 4
   6
   3
   7

Reverse the numbers in the previous column and add 1 to the number at the bottom of that column.

Answers, explanations and assessments

6 HJKN: it follows the pattern Hi JK/*m*N; the rest follow the pattern CdEF*g*H.

7 suppress
reserve

8 D: the dot moves round two places clockwise at each stage and alternates black/white.

9 encyclopedia

10 88 and 55: deduct 5, 7, 9, 11, 13, 15, 17

11 accessory

12 fabulous: it means fanciful or imaginary. The rest mean celebrated or renowned.

13 6: $(19 + 11) \div 5 = 6$; $(13 + 5) \div 3 = 6$

14 A: C is the same as E with large/small circle reversal, and similarly B is the same as D.

15 donate, give

16 910: $5 + 4 = 9, 3 + 7 = 10$

17 augment

18 D

19 literal, verbatim

20 11: $13 + 31 = 44$ and $44 \div 4 = 11$

21 B: the rectangle increases in size and rotates 90°. The square reduces in size and goes inside the figure originally inside the square, which in turn goes inside the rectangle having rotated 180°.

22 E

23 accustomed

24 C: looking across a black dot is added. Looking down a circle is added.

25 51 litres: 5% = 4.25, therefore 40% = 4.25 × 8 = 34. 85 less 34 = 51.

26 crave, dislike

27 A: the number of sides in the figure reduce by 1. The number of dots increase by 1 and turn white to black.

28 76: add 19 each time.

29 F: the large arc rotates 90° clockwise at each stage, the middle arc rotates 90° anti-clockwise at each stage, and the inner arc rotates 90° anti-clockwise at each stage.

30 5: each number in the outer circle is the difference of the two numbers immediately next to it anti-clockwise in the inner circles. So, 9 − 4 = 5, 7 − 5 = 2, 8 − 1 = 7, etc.

31 Switch C is not working.

32 B: the rest are the same figure rotated.

33 6.5: add the numbers in the same position in the left and right circles to obtain the number in the same position in the centre circle.

Answers, explanations and assessments

34 E: only figures that appear in the same position in the first and second squares looking both across and down are carried forward to the final square; however, circles turn to squares and vice versa.

35 nocturnal

36 91: add 11, 12, 13, 14, 15, 16

37 A

38 Joe 36, Mo 24, Flo 16

39 The Gardeners' Association debated whether to hold its bi-annual flower show at the beginning of April and September, or at the end of April and September each year.

40 28: looking across, add 2, 4, 6. Looking down, add 3, 5, 7.

Each completely correct answer scores one point.

Assessment

36–40	Exceptional
31–35	Excellent
25–30	Very good
19–24	Good
15–18	Average

Chapter 2 – Specific aptitude tests

Test 2.1   Synonym test A

Answers

1 adhesive

2 informative

3 adoption

4 connote

5 scholarly

6 nonsensical

7 equanimity

8 extensive

9 lattice

10 overfill

11 assiduously

12 force

13 eager

14 rest

15 calcify

16 epitomize

17 scolding

18 charade

19 tirade

20 custom

Assessment

8–11	Average
12–15	Good
16–17	Very good
18–20	Exceptional

Test 2.2 Synonym test B

Answers

1 gnaw, chew

2 inimitable, matchless

3 recruit, mobilize

4 unchaste, impure

5 workaday, prosaic

6 inveterate, entrenched

7 abandon, relinquish

8 cursory, hurried

9 opinionated, dogmatic

10 orbit, encircle

11 orchestrate, score

12 virulent, noxious

13 yet, moreover

14 sophistic, fallacious

15 assist, facilitate

16 horizontal, supine

17 fare, food

18 guide, shepherd

19 retreat, getaway

20 genre, type

Assessment

8–11	Average
12–15	Good
16–17	Very good
18–20	Exceptional

Test 2.3   Antonym test A

Answers

1 accelerate

2 flexible

3 genteel

4 genial

5 democratic

6 comprehensible

7 compress

8 inconceivable

9 humane

10 tiny

11 adjacent

12 proven

13 mellow

14 ethereal

15 eulogise

16 bold

17 nervous

18 burden

19 appended

20 discordant

Assessment

8–11	Average
12–15	Good
16–17	Very good
18–20	Exceptional

Test 2.4   Antonym test B

Answers

1 murky, bright

2 scarce, profuse

3 contradict, substantiate

4 similar, contrary

5 fluent, faltering

6 salvation, perdition

7 hazardous, secure

8 wasteful, frugal

9 candid, subtle

10 gregarious, unsociable

11 allow, proscribe

12 rear, bow

13 important, petty

14 diplomatic, rude

15 absolve, convict

16 zest, apathy

17 turmoil, calm

18 taut, slack

19 neophyte, instructor

20 phlegmatic, animated

Assessment

8–11	Average
12–15	Good
16–17	Very good
18–20	Exceptional

Test 2.5   Analogy test A

Answers

1 hands

2 obsession

3 astonish

4 stalk

5 fourteen

6 flashes

7 imposing

8 lead

9 panel

10 occident

11 pen

12 use

13 engine

14 swan

15 unbroken

16 blue

17 intersect

18 drill

19 expert

20 realisation

Answers, explanations and assessments

Assessment

8–11	Average
12–15	Good
16–17	Very good
18–20	Exceptional

Test 2.6   Analogy test B

Answers

1 fruit, tree

2 fire, fling

3 fur, plumage

4 night, winter

5 star, ring

6 tongue, legs

7 substances, animals

8 journey, meeting

9 book, opera

10 politician, king

11 furniture, spur

12 gangster, bandit

13 piano, drum

14 animal, verse

15 slow, soft

16 sin, virtue

17 church, hospital

18 regulate, rectify

19 ditch, watchtower

20 grass, mountain

Assessment

8–11	Average
12–15	Good
16–17	Very good
18–20	Exceptional

Test 2.7   Classification test

Answers

1 level: all the others mean straight up.

2 exceptional: all the others mean the very best.

3 covering: the rest are specifically types of closed containers.

4 deceive: the rest mean to persuade.

Answers, explanations and assessments

5 visit: it means to call on, the rest mean to call to.

6 steeple: it is part of a church, the rest all being actual places of worship.

7 buffoonery: it means clowning around, the rest mean nonsensical.

8 perfect: it means 100%, the rest are just OK.

9 spheroid: it is round, the rest are square.

10 discontinue: it means to sign off, the rest mean to sign away.

11 scorched: it means hot, the rest mean dry.

12 certificate: the rest are types of information.

13 burrow: it means to dig, the rest mean to plough.

14 feline: it is a cat, the rest are types of monkey.

15 design: the rest mean to shape.

16 strange: the rest are all unreal.

17 holiday: the rest are specific types of festivity.

18 orbicular: it is going around, the rest go from side to side or sideways.

19 distribute: it means to hand out, the rest mean to hand in.

20 recurrent: it means repeatedly, the rest mean irregularly.

Assessment

8–11	Average
12–15	Good
16–17	Very good
18–20	Exceptional

Test 2.8   Comprehension

Answers

1 Just as the hapless interviewer was half way through asking his
   most involved and difficult question, the worst thing that could
   have happened did, and all hell was let loose as Ben saw a cat
   through the dining room window. Apart from almost barking the
   house down and totally drowning out the second half of the
   question, Ben shot across the dining room in a brown blur before
   throwing himself against the kitchen door with a sickening crash.

2 We all have the potential to be creative, however, because of the
   pressures of modern living and the need for specialization, many
   of us never have the time or opportunity, or indeed are given the
   encouragement, to explore our latent talents, even though most
   of us have sufficient ammunition to realise this potential in the
   form of data which has been fed into, collated and processed by
   the brain over many years.

3 Learning is the acquisition of new knowledge, and memory is the
   retention of this knowledge. The combination of learning and
   memory, therefore, is the basis of all our knowledge and abilities
   and is what enables us to consider the past, exist in the present
   and plan for the future.

Answers, explanations and assessments

Assessment

Each correct answer scores one point.

12–16	Average
17–27	Good
28–40	Very good
41–45	Exceptional

Test 2.9   Advanced verbal test A – multi-discipline

Answers

1 The school *principal* tried to persuade the police not to *prosecute* the boys for what had been a *momentary* lapse in their good behaviour.

2 sincerity

3 surveillance

4 whimsical

5 appreciative

6 renounce, disclaim

7 sporadic, frequent

8 act the part of

9 avarice

10 There is no single definition of success, as what is considered to be success by one individual may differ considerably for another.

11 When used in dialogue, the question mark is placed inside the quotation marks, and replaces the full stop.

12 The candidate was able to demonstrate his ability to sustain a high level of work activity.

13 liability, hindrance

14 list

15 manner/manor

16 anonymous, incognito

17 sagacious

18 perigee, perihelion

19 literal, fanciful

20 yesterday

21 insomniac

22 undemanding

23 resort

24 austere

25 thrift, profligacy

Assessment

8–11	Average
12–17	Good
18–22	Very good
23–25	Exceptional

Test 2.10   Advanced verbal test B – anagrams

Answers

1 impulse

2 feat, exploit

3 put to sea

4 NBDRA = brand

5 NFEOT = often

6 SHE ELK = shekel; the animals are donkey (OK deny), gopher (hog rep) and badger (garbed).

7 STOREY = oyster; the trees are poplar (rap lop), spruce (PC user) and cherry (her cry).

8 PEOTM = tempo

9 slick, crude

10 gauntlet

11 prepared

12 obstinate

13 alleviate

14 sultana

15 canoe, tanker, ferry

16 pilot, banker, chef

17 cohesion

18 load, cargo

19 obsolete

20 periodical

Assessment

8–10	Average
11–13	Good
14–16	Very good
17–20	Exceptional

Test 2.11   Number sequence test

Answers

1 64: add 1, 3, 5, 7, etc.

2 36, 54: add 9 each time.

3 83.75: deduct 3.25 each time.

4 24, 76: there are two sequences interwoven. Add 6 starting at 0 and deduct 6 starting at 100.

5 85: add 17 each time

6 6: ×1, ×2, ×3, ×4, ×5, ×6

Answers, explanations and assessments

7 58: deduct 2, 4, 6, 8, 10, 12

8 19: add 1.5, 2.5, 3.5, 4.5, 5.5

9 12.5: there are two interwoven sequences, ×2 starting at 100 and ÷2 starting at 50.

10 9.5: add 3.75 each time.

11 75, 26: there are two interwoven sequences, −2.5, −5, −7.5 starting at 100 and +2.5, 5, 7.5 starting at 1.

12 108: deduct the sum of the digits of the previous number each time.

13 26, 31: +1, +1, +2, +2, +3, +3, +4, +4, +5, +5

14 3281: ×5 + 1 each time

15 857: deduct 28.6 each time

16 945: ×1, ×3, ×5, ×7, ×9

17 108: add 36 each time

18 7, 11: there are two interwoven sequences, +1.5 starting at the first 1, and +2.5 starting at the second 1.

19 432, 1296: ×2, ×3, ×2, ×3, ×2, ×3

20 70, 80: there are two interwoven sequences, add 14 starting at 14 and add 16 starting at 16.

Assessment

8–11	Average
12–15	Good
16–17	Very good
18–20	Exceptional

Test 2.12   Mental arithmetic

Answers

1 72

2 42

3 165

4 135

5 14

6 24

7 87.5

8 150

9 61

10 82

11 168

12 64

Answers, explanations and assessments

13 458

14 83

15 176

16 150

17 $\frac{5}{8}$ of 112 = 70; $\frac{7}{8}$ of 88 = 77

18 3706

19 56

20 881

21 101

22 1080

23 0.2

24 198

25 7634

26 852

27 935

28 20.04

29 26.9

30 47.95

Assessment

28–30	Exceptional
24–27	Very good
17–23	Good
10–16	Average

Test 2.13   Working with numbers

Answers

1   13 minutes (11.47): 11.47 less 68 minutes = 10.39. 10 a.m. plus
    39 minutes (3 × 13) = 10.39.

2   Jack 9, Jill 3: in 3 years' time Jack will be 12 and Jill will be 6.

3   Al 24, Sal 36, Mal 54.

4   Alice £62.00, Susan £22.00:

Alice, 62 − 6 = 56   Alice, 62 + 1 = 63
Susan, 22 + 6 = 28   Susan, 22 − 1 = 21

5   300: $(\frac{180}{3}) \times 5 = 300$

6   £140.00: $\frac{2}{5} = 0.4$; 0.4 + 0.45 = 0.85, therefore £21.00 = 0.15 (15%)
    and $\frac{21}{15} \times 100 = 140$.

7   23 units and 12 units: 23 × 12 = 276; (23 + 12) × 2 = 70.

8   350: 250 + 40% = 350

9   2

10   £214.20

Answers, explanations and assessments

11 95 minutes, or 1 hour 35 minutes.

12 80: combined age in 7 years = 92; 4 × 7 = 28, therefore, combined age now is 92 − 28 = 64; in 4 years' time combined age is therefore 64 + 16 (4 × 4) = 80.

13 $\frac{5}{16} + \frac{5}{8}(\frac{10}{16}) = \frac{15}{16}$: $\frac{1}{16}$, therefore, =115 and $\frac{5}{16}$ (5 × 115) or 575 had just bought cosmetics; $\frac{10}{16}$ (10 × 115) or 1150 had just bought clothing.

14 9: 19 × 3 = 57 (total of three numbers); 24 × 2 = 48 (total of two numbers); the third number is therefore 57 − 48 = 9.

15 £3.64: £5.76/12 = 0.48; individually, 0.48 + 0.04 = 0.52, and 0.52 × 7 = £3.64.

16 70 runs: 10 innings @ 15 per innings = 150 total (average 15); 11 innings @ 16 per innings = 176 total (average 16); 11 innings @ 20 per innings = 220 total (average 20); 150 + 70 = 220.

17 1 part = 500: $\frac{4500}{9}$ (2 + 3 + 4); apples 1000, oranges 1500, plums 2000.

18 10 hours: 120 miles @ 20 m.p.h. = 6 hours
      90 miles @ 30 m.p.h. = 3 hours
      9 hours
    plus 1 hour break = 10 hours

19 15 days: the five men take 21 × 5 = 105 man-days to build the house; seven men therefore build the house in 15 days ($\frac{105}{7}$).

20 The number of votes the winning candidate received was (972 + 52 + 78 + 102) ÷ 4 = 301; the second received 301 − 52 = 249; the third received 301 − 78 = 223, and the fourth received 301 − 102 = 199.

Assessment

8–11	Average
12–15	Good
16–17	Very good
18–20	Exceptional

Test 2.14   Advanced numerical aptitude test

Answers

1 26: start at the top number in each group and spiral anti-clockwise, finishing in the centre. The numbers in the first group increase by 2, in the second group by 3, in the third group by 4 and in the fourth group by 5.

2 97. 5 kg: 100% less 35% = 65%, less 20% = 52%, less 25% = 39%; 39% × 250 = 97.5.

3 6, 15: there are two interwoven sequences: 10, 9, 8, 7, 6 and 11, 12, 13, 14, 15.

4 42: $(6 \times 6) + 6$

5 50%: it is a certainty that at least two coins will fall with the same side up. Thus it is just as likely that these two coins will be tails as it is they will be heads.

6 2 minutes 12 seconds:

$$(2.5 + 0.25) \times \frac{60}{75} = 2.75 \times \frac{60}{75} = 2.2 \text{ minutes or 2 minutes 12 seconds.}$$

7 11: $[(23 + 15) - 5] \div 3$

Answers, explanations and assessments

8 50: add 1, 3, 9, 27, 81, i.e. the amount added is multiplied by 3 each time.

9 12: $9 \times 5 \times 12 = 540$

10 18, 68: add the three numbers in each row and column to obtain the fourth number.

11 Seven bags each containing 13 apples: 91 is the product of two prime numbers, 7 and 13.

12 £40.70: train £27.35 + taxi £11.45(27.35 − 15.90) + bus £1.90(11.45 − 9.55) = £40.70.

13 343: each number is the cube of the number of sides of the figure in which it is contained ($7 \times 7 \times 7 = 343$).

14 46.75 square metres: I have 240 square metres ($20 \times 4 = 80$ sq m $\times 3 = 240$) ($6 \times 18 = 108$) + ($15.5 \times 5.5 = 85.25$) = 193.25; $240 - 193.25 = 46.75$.

15 9: $\frac{1}{4}$ or $\frac{4}{16}$ took sugar only $+ \frac{5}{8}$ or $\frac{10}{16}$ took milk and sugar $+ \frac{1}{16}$ took milk only $= \frac{15}{16}$; the remainder, $\frac{1}{16}$, took it black; $\frac{144}{16} = 9$.

Assessment

6–7	Average
8–10	Good
11–12	Very good
13–15	Exceptional

Test 2.15   Technical aptitude test

Answers

1 Of the nine faces shown (or 18 half-faces), six out of 18 half-faces are shaded. One-third of the total figure visible is therefore shaded.

2

2

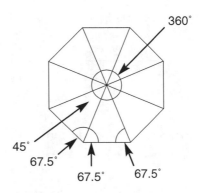

The value of the circle shown in the middle is 360°. The value of each segment is therefore 45° (360 ÷ 8); the remaining angles, therefore, are equal to 180 − 45 = 135 or 67.5° each (180° being the sum of the internal angles of a triangle); each internal angle is therefore 135°.

3 f) zinc and copper

4 c) heating it

5 d) parallelepiped

6 6.75 sq units:

$$2.75 \times 0.75 = 2.0625$$
$$1 \times 0.75 = 0.75$$
$$5.25 \times 0.75 = \underline{3.9375}$$
$$6.75$$

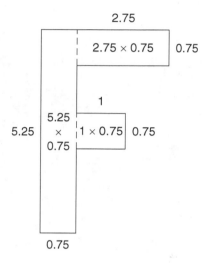

7 AB = diameter, CD = radius, EF = chord, GH = secant.

8 *Conduction* is when heat travels from the warmed end of an object towards the cool end. *Radiation* is when heat travels through space. *Convection* is when heat from a hotplate is transferred to water in a pan placed on the hotplate.

9 c) force

10 b) 740 m.p.h.

11 e) 20 hexagons and 12 pentagons

12 50: 12 at the back, 10 at the sides, 6 underneath, 6 on top, 12 at the front, 4 on the insides.

13 c) Pythagoras' theorem

14 224

15 b) Hertz

Assessment

6–7	Average
8–10	Good
11–12	Very good
13–15	Exceptional

Chapter 3 – Logical reasoning

Test 3.1   Pure logic

Answers

1 tortoise: the name of each creature commences with the letter that come two letters in the alphabet after the last letter of the previous creature. Also the name of each creature contains one more letter than the previous creature.

2 October: jump an extra month each time, i.e. January February (March) April (May June) July (August September October) November (December January February March) April (May June July August September) October.

3 D   I
   S   N

   Starting letters for each square, commencing at the top left-hand corner, are ABCD. Each square jumps an extra letter, rotating clockwise. AbCdEfG, BcdEfgHijK, CdefGhijKlmnO, DefghIjklmNopqrS.

4 583796: the bottom three rows are the reverse of the top three rows of numbers.

5 10 and 6: opposite pairs of numbers in the first circle total 11, in the second circle they total 12, and in the third circle 13.

6 9
   4
   7
   5

   The numbers reading down the middle are the sum of the top and bottom numbers in another figure; 5821 + 3654 = 9475.

7 2681749: reverse the first three numbers, then reverse the last four numbers.

8
3859	1114	25
4978	1315	46
7579	1216	37

$3 + 8 = 11, 5 + 9 = 14$ $1 + 1 = 2, 1 + 4 = 5$

9 16: $(33 + 31) \div 4 = 16$

10 76: reverse the first number but discard the highest and lowest digits.

Assessment

4–5	Average
6–7	Good
8	Very good
9–10	Exceptional

Test 3.2 Progressive matrices test

Answers

1 B: the diamond is shown pointing north, south, east and west.

2 E: the lines within the large square are drawn top, bottom, middle left and middle bottom.

3 A: looking down, the large circle disappears, and looking across, the smaller middle circle disappears.

Answers, explanations and assessments

4 F: each line across and down contains one triangle upside down, one circle, and one set of vertical lines.

5 B: looking across and down only, lines (and the circle) which appear in the same position twice in the first two squares are carried forward to the final square.

6 E: looking across and down, any lines that appear in the same position twice in the first two squares are cancelled out in the final square.

7 G: only dots of the same colour which appear in the same position twice in the first two squares are carried forward to the final square; however, they then change from black to white and vice versa.

8 C: so that each vertical and horizontal line contains one each of the four different circle combinations.

9 F: so that the first and third lines are the same as are the second and fourth lines.

10 B: looking across and down, alternate circle combinations are repeated with the addition of an extra circle.

Assessment

Each correct answer scores one point

4–5	Average
6–7	Good
8	Very good
9–10	Exceptional

Test 3.3 Advanced logic test

Answers

1 74: the numbers 1 37 4 9 32 5 68 1 appear in the same order, reading clockwise around the outer and inner sections of the heptagon.

2 129: $5\mathit{3} - 4\mathit{4}$; $3 \times 4 = 12$ and $5 + 4 = 9$

3 8492: The numbers in the bottom rectangle are formed by taking digits from opposite pairs of numbers in the top rectangle, e.g. the digits *38***29** and **48***73*, produce the numbers *7338* and **8492** in the bottom rectangle.

4 humane: the words have alternate consonant/vowel arrangement, starting with a consonant.

5 It was Ernie. If the statements are set out as in the table below, it is seen that only Ernie has three ticks against his name, which means that if it was Ernie, just three statements, those of Ben, Dave and Ernie, are correct.

Culprit	Statements				
	Alf	Ben	Charlie	Dave	Ernie
Alf		✓	✓	✓	✓
Ben			✓	✓	
Charlie		✓	✓	✓	✓
Dave	✓	✓	✓		✓
Ernie		✓		✓	✓

✓ = Correct.

6 60587

Answers, explanations and assessments

7

5	7	8	6	8	6
8	6	3	5	7	4
2	4	7	8	6	8
5	8	6	4	5	7
3	1	7	2	8	6
7	4	8	5	7	3

The grid contains 1×1, 2×2, 3×3, 4×4, 5×5, 6×6, 7×7 and 8×8. All numbers are placed in the grid so that the same two numbers are never in adjacent squares, either horizontally, vertically or diagonally.

8 C: A is the same figure as E and B is the same figure as D.

9 You have drunk exactly the same amount of coffee as you have drunk milk. The cup originally contained coffee only; you have poured in one-third + one-half + one-sixth, which adds up to 1. You have therefore poured into the cup exactly the same amount of milk as the coffee and have, in effect, drunk one full cup of coffee and one full cup of milk.

10 Take one ball from bag 1, two balls from bag 2, three balls from bag 3, four balls from bag 4 and five balls from bag 5. Place all 15 balls on the scale. The scale would register $150 \times 20 = 3000$ grams if all balls weighed 20 grams. If the scale registers 2998 grams, then the balls in bag 1 are light; if the scale registers 2996, the balls in bag 2 are light; if the scale registers 2994, it is the balls in bag 3; if the scale registers 2992, it is the balls in bag 4; and if the scale registers 2990, it is the balls in bag 5 that are light.

Assessment

4–5	Average
6–7	Good
8	Very good
9–10	Exceptional

Chapter 4 – Creativity

Test 4.0   Creativity personality test

Assessment

Total score 90–125

This score indicates a high degree of creativity and means that the right, creative, side of your brain appears to be extremely active.

People who are creative in nature are likely to have tried out many different pursuits during their lifetime and will continue to do so in the coming years, as they are never afraid of trying out something new. It is even possible that you have already achieved some degree of success and fulfilment within a creative environment, e.g. as a writer or designer.

It is suggested that people who have achieved a high score on this test, but who have not yet experimented with creative pursuits such as painting, garden or interior design or music, should follow their intuition and do so now, whatever their age, since they appear to have the necessary qualities, which possibly have been lying dormant, to achieve success and fulfilment in some sort of creative pursuit.

While it is difficult to be too creative, people who have scored highly on this test should not overlook the importance of developing their analytical and intellectual skills, as well as their creative talents.

Total score 65–89

This score indicates an average degree of creativity.

Although you may exhibit creative tendencies, a score at the lower end of this group suggests it is possible you may have neither the time nor the confidence to try out new creative pursuits. In order to become more creative it may be necessary to develop more confidence and be more relaxed about taking intellectual risks, such as sitting down and doing some drawing or painting, or making a start on writing the novel you always felt was inside you.

A score within the higher range of this group suggests that you may have already achieved some degree of creative success, but that you may also have major undeveloped talents waiting to surface and be cultivated.

Generally, however, any score within this group does suggest you are in the fortunate position of being able to balance your creative tendencies with logical and analytically formed judgements in order to turn many of your ideas into a single, realistic and workable concept.

Total score less than 65

Although this score indicates a lower than average degree of creative talents there may be many reasons for this, e.g. while you may possess a rich storehouse of ideas, it may be that you feel more comfortable when guided by set principles and traditional conventions.

Although each one of us has the potential to be creative in some way or other, it may be that, like many other people, you have not yet explored your creative talents.

It is quite likely that your skill outlets have been channelled into one particular area in order to develop a career, and as such you are a specialist who has little time to explore other avenues.

Creativity and intellect are two quite separate brain functions and it is thus entirely possible to be highly intellectual in some fields but not creative, and vice versa. It is, however, possible to train yourself to bring out latent creative talents if you have the time and inclination to do so. By exploring new avenues and learning experiences it is possible to broaden your horizons considerably, and possibly surprise yourself by discovering you possess creative talents and aptitudes of which you were previously unaware.

Test 4.1   Imaginative shapes

Assessment

You can mark this test yourself; however, it is best marked by a friend or family member. Award one mark for each recognisable sketch, provided that it is not similar to any of the other sketches. For example, if you draw a face, a second face scores no points as each sketch must have an original theme. You thus obtain marks for variety. If you are creative, you will tend to try to draw something different for each sketch.

There is no one correct answer to any of the eight sketches as for each there is any number of ideas.

3–4   Average
5–6   Good
7–8   Very creative
9   Exceedingly creative

Repeat the exercise as many times as you wish. Try other geometric objects or lines as a starting point.

Test 4.3   Creative logic

Answers

1 C: the rest are the same figure rotated.

2 D: so that the dot appears in the diamond and two circles.

3 B: the black dots increase by 1 each time and alternate top/bottom. The white dots decrease by 1 each time and alternate bottom/top.

4 B: every alternate circle contains a dot, every fourth circle contains lines middle of top and bottom; starting at the second circle, every alternate circle contains a right bottom line and starting at the third circle every fourth circle contains a right top line.

5 F: looking at rows and columns, in each horizontal and vertical line of dots, just one in each line of three dots appears black in each row and column.

Answers, explanations and assessments

6 B: Only lines that appear in the same position just twice in the four surrounding circles are transferred to the centre circle.

7 D: A is the same as F with black/white dot reversal. Similarly, B is the same as E and C is the same as G.

8 E: the rest are the same figure rotated.

9 E: the box with the black border is the combination of the remaining three boxes in the same row, except where lines appear in the same position in any of these three boxes, in which case they are cancelled out.

10 D: the rest are the same figure rotated.

Assessment

4–5	Average
6–7	Good
8	Very good
9–10	Exceptional

Test 4.4   The bucket test

Assessment

You can self-evaluate this test; however, it is best marked by a friend or family member.

The following scores should be awarded:

- 2 points for any good, original, or useful answer.
- 1 point for not-so-good answers that nevertheless constitute a good attempt.
- 0 points for completely impractical answers.
- 0 points for anti-social answers, such as hitting someone over the head with the bucket.

16–20 points   Highly creative and imaginative mind
12–15 points   Good effort
 7–11 points   Average

Test 4.5   Lateral thinking test

Answers

1 E
  T
  A

Read up each column in turn in each square to spell out the words 'carpentry', 'redevelop' and 'candidate'.

2 prisoners: the letters 'one' appear in the sequence one******, *one*****, **one****, ***one***, ****one**.

3 922: $107 + 236 = 343$, $236 + 343 = 579$, $343 + 579 = 922$.

4 J: Each group is a set of alternate letters of the alphabet, FgHiJkL.

5 9: the totals of the columns decrease; 9, 8, 7, 6, 5.

6 Just one: the one in the middle. No other circles appear, just arcs.

7 L: to spell BAGEL. Take the first letter on the top row with the last letter on the bottom row, etc., which plus the AGE in the middle spell out BAGEL, PAGER, LAGER, CAGEY, WAGED, EAGER and RAGES.

8 85: reverse the numbers at the top and add 1 to the digit originally on the left.

9 G: so that the letters inside the triangle can be rearranged to spell the word 'triangle'.

10 9: it is the number of straight lines in each word.

Assessment

4–5	Average
6–7	Good
8	Very good
9–10	Exceptional

Test 4.6 Lateral thinking exercises

Answers

1

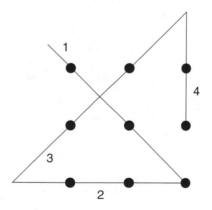

Many people have difficulty with this type of question because they do not think of using the space outside the boundary of the dots.

2 HTSI: eigHT; SIx

3

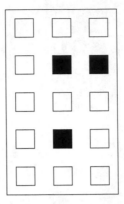

Look at the white squares only and the numbers 2 4 6 8 will appear.

4 The word: wholesome

5 2: every other set is a mirror image of its adjacent set, to the left, right, above or below.

6

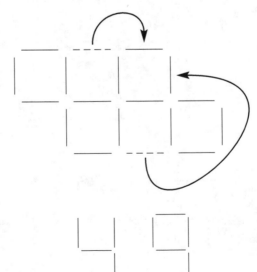

7

The numbers 4, 9 and 49 are all squares.

8 He falls off the edge inwards onto the top of the roof, rather than onto the road below.

9

Turn the page onto its side and look at the figures from the right-hand side. The letters K L M N will appear. The next in sequence is therefore O.

10 insatiable: the abbreviated letters of the week appear in the words:

*sun*flower, a*mon*g, sta*tue*tte, S*wed*en, en*thu*siasm, be*fri*end and in*sat*iable

Test 4.7 Problem-solving exercises

Answers

1 Weigh yourself. Then pick up the puppy and weigh yourself again, but this time holding the puppy. The difference between the two weighings is the weight of the puppy.

2 You ask to die of old age and natural causes.

3

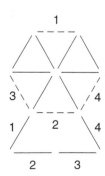

4 Amy was born just before midnight on February 28 and Matthew was born just after midnight on March 1. The year in question is a leap year, so that February 29 falls in between their birthdays.

5

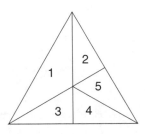

Number the segments 1–5. Triangles are formed by the following segments or combinations:

1, 2, 3, 4, 5, 1–2, 1–3, 2–5, 3–4, 2–5–4, 3–4–5, 1–2–3–4–5.

So, in total there are 12 triangles.

6

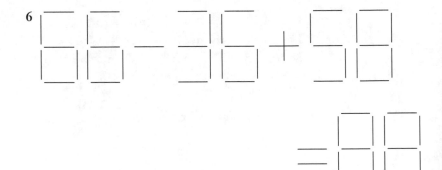

7

8

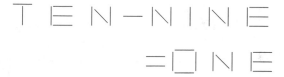

9 The gladiator quickly swallows the piece of paper he picks and offers the other to the emperor, saying, 'Show this paper to the crowd and tell me what I picked and what will be my fate'. Since the eaten one says 'death', in order to save face with the crowd, the emperor has to concede that the paper chosen by the gladiator says 'freedom'.

10

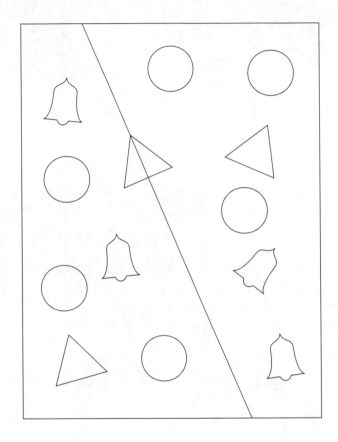

Chapter 6 – Memory

Test 6.1   Pattern recognition A

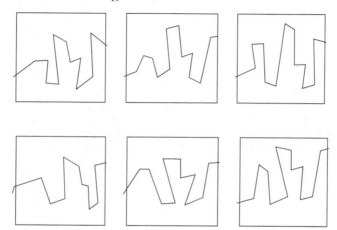

Test 6.2   Association

Question

    ARROW ....
    CHAIR ....
    COMPUTER ....
    SAUSAGE ....
    PENCIL ....
    BALLOON ....
    ROBOT ....
    PARROT ....
    BAGPIPES ....
    TELEVISION ....
    BRIDGE ....
    SNAKE ....
    DICTIONARY ....
    BLACKBOARD ....
    POTATO ....

SLIPPER ....
TREE ....
MOUSTACHE ....
PARASOL ....
NAIL ....
CANDLE ....
TRACTOR ....
PIPE ....
MANDOLIN ....

Put a letter A against one pair, the letter B against a second pair, etc., through to the letter L, until you have matched what you think are the original 12 pairs of words.

Assessment

10–12 pairs correct	Exceptionally good
9	Very good
7–8	Well above average
6	Above average
4–5	Average

Test 6.3   Verbal dexterity and memory test – anagrams

Answers

1 ABSTAIN

2 DOLPHIN

3 UTOPIAN

4 MERMAID

5 LEAFLET

6 POSTURE

7 BROADEN

8 CONCEPT

9 EPISODE

10 VETERAN

11 PARAGON

12 HEARSAY

13 THEOREM

14 OPTIMAL

15 GRIMACE

16 CITIZEN

17 OUTDATE

18 ECONOMY

19 NATURAL

20 AVIATOR

Assessment

Each correct answer scores one point.

17–20	Exceptional
14–16	Very good
11–13	Good
8–10	Average

Test 6.4   Number/shape recognition

Question

1 Which shape is in the middle position?

  a) circle
  b) square
  c) rectangle

2 The letter P appears inside which shape?

  a) rectangle
  b) pentagon
  c) circle

3 Which shape is immediately to the left of the rectangle?

  a) square
  b) pentagon
  c) hexagon

4 In which shape does the letter H appear?

  a) circle
  b) pentagon
  c) rectangle

5 Which letter appears inside the hexagon?

  a) H
  b) A
  c) S

6 Which letter appears inside the square?

  a) S
  b) P
  c) E

7 Which letter is positioned next to the letter A?

   a) S
   b) P
   c) H

8 What word is spelled out by the first three letters in reverse?

   a) ASP
   b) SPA
   c) SHE

9 What word is spelled out by the last three letters?

   a) ASP
   b) SPA
   c) SHE

10 What word is spelled out by taking the third, second, fifth, fourth and first letters, in that order?

   a) PHASE
   b) SHAPE
   c) HEAPS

Assessment

9–10	Exceptional
8	Very good
6–7	Good
4–5	Average

Test 6.5   Pattern recognition B

Question

Which of the following figures did you look at 5 minutes ago on page 147?

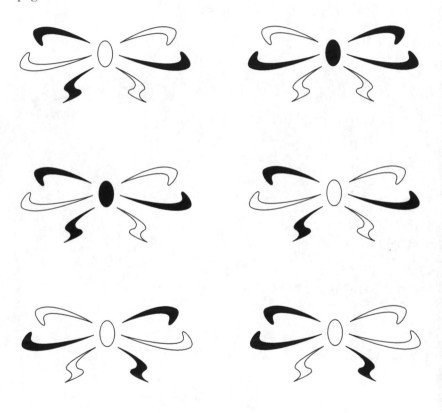

Test 6.6 Instructions

Question

Which of the following sets of instructions have you just looked at on page 148?

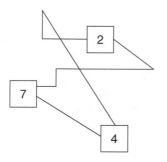

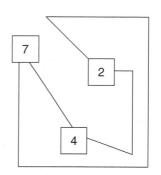

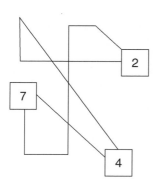

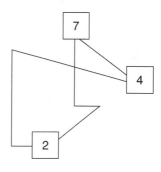

Test 6.7   Pattern recognition C

Question

Which of the following did you look at 2 minutes ago on page 148?

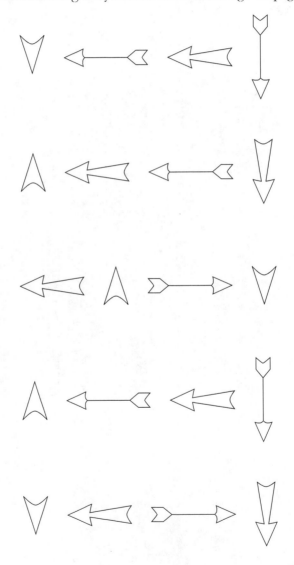

Answers, explanations and assessments

Test 6.8   Shopping list

Question

Write out the 10 items on the shopping list. The order is not important.

Assessment

10	Exceptionally good
9	Very good
7–8	Well above average
5–6	Above average
3–4	Average

Test 6.9   Attention to detail

Questions

1 The arrow is pointing to which letter?

2 How many triangles appear in the drawing?

3 What letter is inside the circle?

4 To what shape is the black circle connected?

5 The letter P appears inside which shape?

6 Three numbers appear in the diagram – what do they add up to?

7 What shape appears immediately above the number 9?

8 How many squares appear in the drawing?

Assessment

7–8	Exceptional
6	Very good
5	Good
4	Average

Test 6.10   Memorising an address

Question

Fill in the 10 blank spaces to complete the address as accurately as possible:

David ******* Christiensen
*th Floor
******* House
*** Osprey Drive ****
off ************** Lane
****** lee
*** ingham
JU** 9**

Assessment

9–10	Exceptional
8	Very good
6–7	Good
4–5	Average

8 Hints

Test 2.10, question 3: depart.

Test 4.5, question 2: look for a word pattern that is occurring throughout each of the words.

Test 4.6, question 2: look at letter spellings.

Test 4.6, question 3: numerical sequence.

Test 4.6, question 5: mirror image.

Test 4.6, question 7: square numbers?

Test 4.6, question 10: the seventh word completes the list.

Test 4.7, question 7: try finding a solution standing on your head!

Test 4.7, question 10: make two triangles out of one.